HOW TO DRAW
B I R D S

MORE BIRDS
TO DRAW

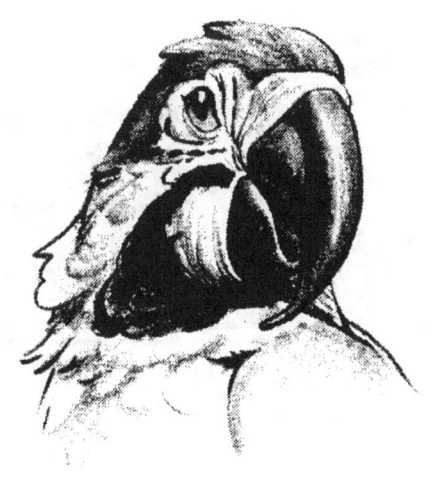

HOW TO DRAW
BIRDS
~by~ RAYMOND SHEPPARD

HOW TO DRAW
BIRDS

MORE BIRDS
TO DRAW

RAYMOND SHEPPARD

COACHWHIP PUBLICATIONS
Greenville, Ohio

How to Draw Birds & More Birds to Draw, by Raymond Sheppard
© 2018 Coachwhip Publications

Published 1940 and 1956
No claims made on public domain material.

CoachwhipBooks.com

ISBN 1-61646-440-2
ISBN-13 978-1-61646-440-0

HOW TO DRAW
BIRDS

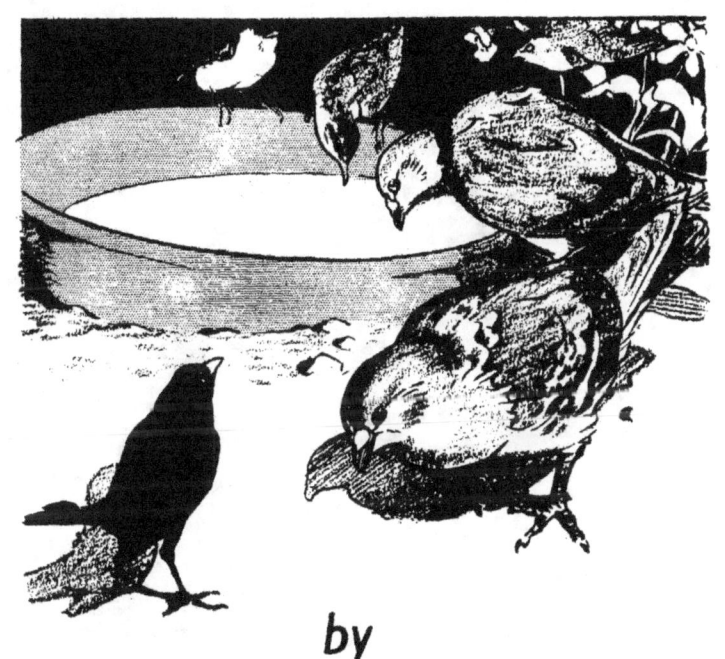

by

RAYMOND SHEPPARD

CONTENTS

Page

Introduction 5
A Method of Approach 10
    Mute Swan 11
A Talk about Anatomy and Construction 17
    Skeleton of Bird 18
Wings, Feathers and Flight 19
    Bones and Feathers 21
    Types of Wings 23
    Tail Feathers 25
Beaks 26
    Types of Beaks 27
Feet 28
    Types of Feet 29
Ducks 30
    Drawings of Ducks 31
Ducks in the Water 32
    Drawings of Ducks in the Water 33
Well-known Birds seen from the Breakfast Table .. 34
    Missel Thrush 35
    Thrushes, Redwings and Blackbird 37
Starlings 38
    Studies of Starlings 39
Birds of Wood and Hedgerow 40
    Blackcap 41
    Nuthatch 42
    Bullfinch 43

Oyster-Catcher and Curlew 44
    Studies of Oyster-Catcher and Curlew 45
Heron 46
    Studies of Heron 47
Kingfisher 48
    Studies of Kingfisher 49
Partridge 50
    Studies of Partridges 51
Domestic Fowl 52
    Cockerels 53
Raven 54
    Studies of a Raven 55
Three Birds of Prey—Barn Owl, Buzzard and Golden Eagle 56
    Barn Owl 57
    Common Buzzard 58
    Golden Eagle 59
On the Wing—Gull, Duck, Swallow and Kestrel .. 60
    Herring Gull and Black-backed Gull 61
    Wild Duck 62
    Swallows 63
    Kestrel 64

INTRODUCTION

Quite recently I was asked by someone, why I liked drawing birds so much. Well, I had never really considered why—I just drew them, but when you really come to think of it, you know, there are a lot of amazing and interesting things about birds that most people don't realise.

Just think of all the varieties of plumage, in what lovely patterns this is arranged, on some birds so indescribably delicate. But did you know that all this pattern, so lovely in itself, is there to serve the bird a very useful purpose? It is really a sort of camouflage, about which we have heard such a lot recently, a " protective coloration " which merges itself into the bird's natural background of rushes, grass or stones, and as long as the bird is motionless it is invisible to its enemies. I expect our camouflage experts have learnt a lot from the study of these protective patterns and colours of birds. This colour, too, is never quite the same. I was watching some lapwings the other day by a lakeside, and sometimes their dark backs appeared

5

quite grey, and then perhaps the light would catch one, and it seemed to glisten like shot silk with purples and greens.

Those big aeroplanes which fly overhead look rather like great birds, don't they? You see, the men who design them have been studying the shape and flow of lines of a bird, which they call its streamline, and they have tried to adapt these shapes to the designs because they know that birds are the most perfectly streamlined creatures in the world. But I am afraid man has got a long way to go before he produces a flying machine as efficient as some of the birds. Look at the sea-gull, how easily he floats on effortless wings. Throw a piece of bread in the air and he swoops with the precision of a Spitfire. Of course man will never be able to invent a covering for his aeroplanes which is as efficient as the birds—I mean feathers. Nothing else we know of combines such lightness and flexibility with such strength. It is these wonderful things,—feathers—which make it possible for such a heavy bird as the swan to fly many thousands of miles on migrating. You would never dream this possible to see him waddling along the ground like something out of a Silly Symphony.

Aren't there a lot of exciting things to know about birds? You know, the more you watch and observe them as they go about their ordinary—I should say extraordinary—lives, the more amazing and wonderful things you will find out about them. I don't know of any other living creatures who are so much the masters of every element. Why, some ducks, besides being very strong flyers, not only swim on the water but under it as well and dive and walk! Of course to be able to do this they have developed perfectly and beautifully shaped bodies. It must take a very quick little brain to control the energy required for such rapid and varied action. This bright bird-brain looks at you from every avian eye. No wonder that all through the ages mankind has been absorbed and fascinated by the study of bird-life.

On the temple walls of ancient Egypt you may see carvings and low reliefs of the birds men venerated and worshipped for three thousand years. Ages ago in China, artists had captured for ever on silk, graceful attitude and delicate pattern. Monuments to the eternal appeal of birds are these lovely relics, caught in still attitude upon the ageless stone and silk.

I think that the real reason I like so much drawing birds is not entirely because I am so interested in their lives and actions, but more so because of the innumerable patterns I can make out of their so varied and graceful movements, the limitless groupings, arrangements and placings of curves and lines and shapes that arise from their ever-varying postures. It is so exciting trying to get just the right lines, to suggest an attitude or rhythm momentarily observed, be it fluent line of swan or heron, or rugged squareness of the eagle. Art and beauty are so inseparably woven together, and birds are undoubtedly the most perfectly formed of living creatures.

Wouldn't you like to be able to draw them yourself? There is nothing to stop you, because the whole secret of drawing is learning to " see properly," and we all have two eyes, so that once you have learnt to observe and use your eyes properly you too can get started on this fascinating study of drawing from the living bird. The trouble with most beginners is that they see too much. By too much I mean they become absorbed in details of plumage and delicate pattern before they have learnt to see those big simple shapes upon the *surface of which* these accessories are placed. Consequently they produce a flat feathered map of a bird.

I have devoted a part of this little book to explaining the basic form and construction of a bird, the few simple masses in which the feathers are arranged. And once you have got interested in these things and learnt what few important facts to look for, it will surprise you what fun you will get out of drawing from living, moving birds.

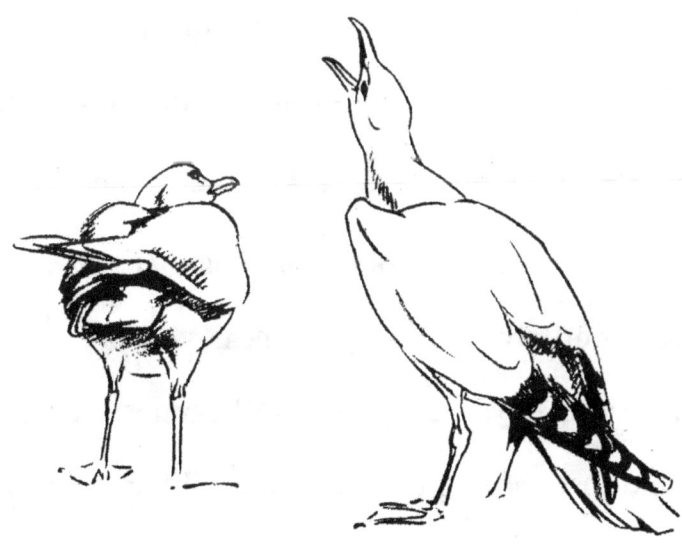

A METHOD OF APPROACH

Most people I have talked to about drawing birds have said that "it must be very difficult because birds move so quickly and never keep still." These people, of course, are thinking about the way they have been taught to draw such subjects as still-life groups or a posed model, where they are told to close one eye, hold a pencil at arm's length, and measure up relative proportions that they are unable to judge with their own unaided eyes. This method is bad in any sort of drawing (it makes you see things as 'flat' not round objects, and leads to an expressionless sort of copying) and in our sort of drawing *i.e.*, moving, living birds, it is of course a quite impossible method. Well, you say, just how am I to tackle the subject?

You will remember in the introduction I said that drawing is really learning to "see properly," "But," I hear you protest, "I can see probably quite as well as you can, but I still cannot draw!" Perhaps I should have said that 'seeing properly' is really knowing what to look for. The reason your drawing is not good is probably because when you look at a bird your eye is full of a lot of really unimportant details

MUTE SWAN

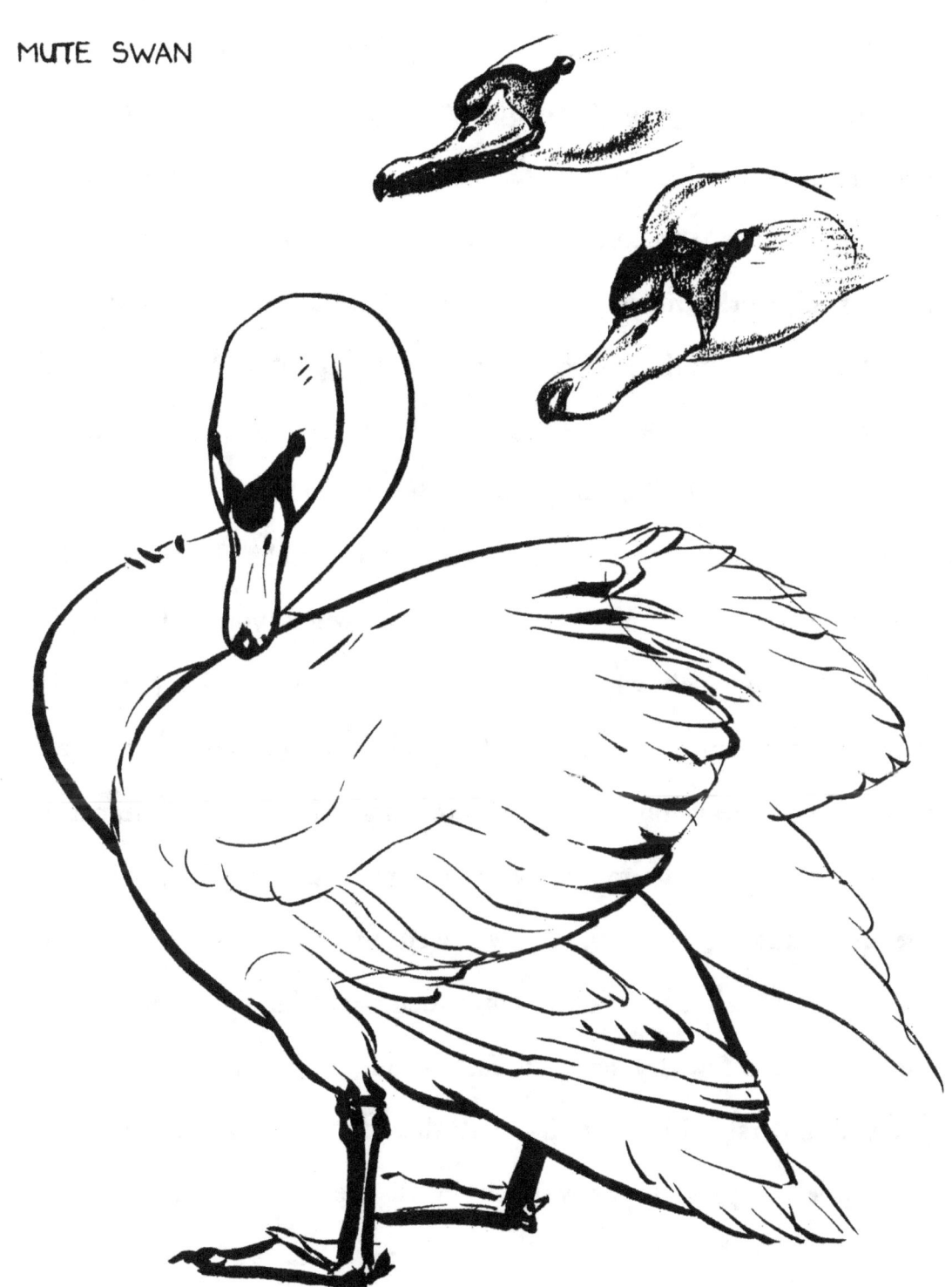

of plumage and small shapes. Now it takes quite a lot of study to be able to " see properly " and quickly too, the important shapes and main lines or rhythms of a pose. So I have told you a little about anatomy, that is, the construction of birds. After all, if you know how a wing works, for instance, your birds are far more likely to look as if they could fly than if you know nothing about such matters. If you know that feathers are arranged in big masses which can be easily seen, that differently shaped beaks are differently shaped for a reason, your drawings will look more convincing, more real. There are a lot more intensely interesting facts about birds which you will probably find out for yourself when you are watching them. They all help your understanding of the shape of the bird, in deciding what to put in and what to leave out in your drawing, and when you have learnt to do this you are well on the way towards " seeing properly " and therefore drawing properly. I say " well on the way to," because of course there is a lot more in drawing such beautiful creatures as birds than noticing a few dry scientific facts about their construction. But you will understand by now that with these facts in your head you are far better equipped to draw birds in all their charm and grace of movement, in all their subtlety of line, than if you were without such knowledge. I do not suggest, however, that you set yourself the 'task' of learning anatomy like you would a lesson at school, for drawing is not a subject that can be taught like a school-room lesson—it is a subject to enjoy, and you will soon discover what an exciting adventure it will become. So refer to the anatomical part of this book, just when you feel the need to—look for the things I have pointed out on the birds themselves. Look and observe—look and observe and draw—and draw—and draw again. That is the way, the interesting way too, to learn.

You know, it isn't really a disadvantage at all that your models (the birds) are always moving and changing their 'poses.' You should take advantage of these changes and instead of trying to do a set drawing of just one pose that may be really quite ordinary and dull—like those awfully boring and tedious sort of " feathered maps " of birds, generally standing stiffly sideways, and looking as flat as pancakes in Natural History books—take a large sheet of paper pinned to a board and make a lot of drawings. Each time the bird moves start a fresh drawing. You will find that the bird will often take up a former attitude again and you can resume drawing on any of your studies at once. You will learn far more about birds in this way, and produce drawings that are more interesting—that look alive. If I were you, I shouldn't use a lot of elaborate shading, at least not to start with. Try looking hard at the bird and noticing what are the main lines of a pose and put them down in free, long strokes. It will surprise you how a few lines can suggest such a lot. I have tried to show you in some of my own studies how a few lines are sometimes all that is necessary to hit off a pose.

Did you realise that every time you look at the bird and then look at your sheet of paper and make a line you are using your memory? To start with you will only remember a little for a very short time, but as you get to know more and have more practice you will find yourself able to remember a lot more for a great deal longer. It is this ability to memorise which will enable you to draw birds in action, especially in flight, when 'sight' drawing is out of the question. So practise memory drawing a lot : it will help you to remember important things.

Sometimes, of course, you will come across birds at rest or asleep—perhaps basking in the sun. Cormorants and shags often stand motionless with wings half-outstretched, as though it were so much washing hung out to dry !

Details such as beaks and feet, and particularly eyes—should be seized upon for study. An outstretched wing of a basking bird presents an opportunity for solving the problem of its foreshortening.

For rapid sketching it doesn't matter what you draw with—whether it be pen, pencil or chalk—it is the " rightness " of what is put down that matters. The drawings reproduced in this book were done, for the most part, with a carbon pencil on cartridge paper—but any paper will do. It is only by experimenting with different mediums that you will find the one which suits your own personal taste.

Now I am going to talk to you about what is really the most important thing in any drawing. It is what artists call " Feeling." By " feeling " I mean that quality in your drawing which shows that you have yourself had an exciting experience, that you have felt wonder at the flowing rhythm, the springing life that is the bird. In short, you show evidence of using your imagination.

When you draw an eagle, try, in imagination, to be an eagle—you are the claws that grasp so firmly—the hooked, cruel beak, and the unquenchable fire that is the sheathed and stabbing glance of the King of Birds. If you can do this, almost unconsciously this will show in your drawing and make of it a work of art, a thing of beauty. This " feeling " is really the emotion you feel—that peculiar, unexplainable tightening inside that makes you want to laugh sometimes, sometimes to sing and dance for joy, and sometimes just a little sad. This is the most important thing of all to cherish, so do not pore over this or any book over long—Rush out into the sunshine—Art does not grow in dusty rooms and is not to be found by searching through books by learned men. No, it is under the great arch of heaven in the pure and sparkling air, through which on wondrous pinions fly the birds we draw, and you in your imagination can fly with them into what unknown and pleasant regions of the mind, to that perfection of Beauty towards which all art aspires.

A TALK ABOUT ANATOMY AND CONSTRUCTION

To start with I am going to talk about the general shape of a bird, and how the various parts of its body work.

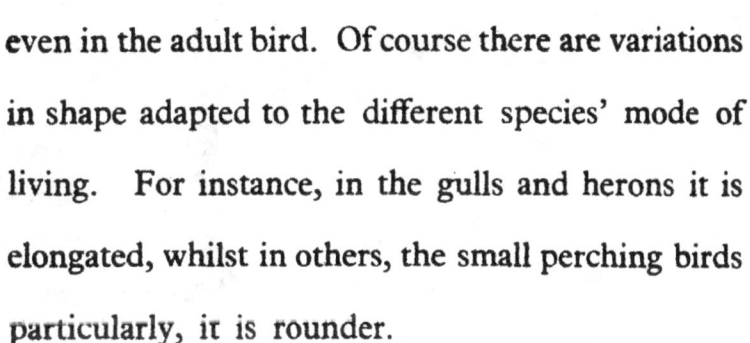

You all know that a bird comes from an egg, and consequently a baby bird is shaped rather like an egg too. Indeed the bird's body retains this egg-like form even in the adult bird. Of course there are variations in shape adapted to the different species' mode of living. For instance, in the gulls and herons it is elongated, whilst in others, the small perching birds particularly, it is rounder.

A bird's body is built like our own on a bony framework. Although most of the bones correspond to ours they have become welded together into one solid framework. It has far more bones in the neck than we have, which gives the bird a far more flexible neck than animals or man.

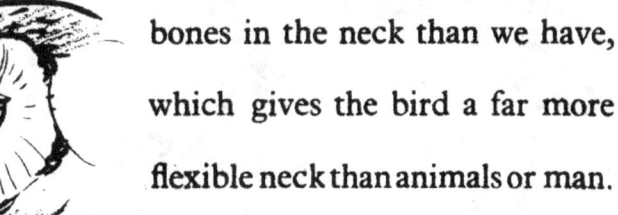

The skull is nearly all eye-socket, and you will notice that pigeons, ducks, sparrows, etc. have the eyes placed on each side of the skull so that they can see all round them, whereas those birds that prey upon them have their eyes set more nearly in front.

In the drawing of the bird's bones, the black parts, *i.e.*, the neck, legs, and bones of wing, are the only movable parts. The body is, as I have said, built on a solid bony framework. This I have shaded in grey.

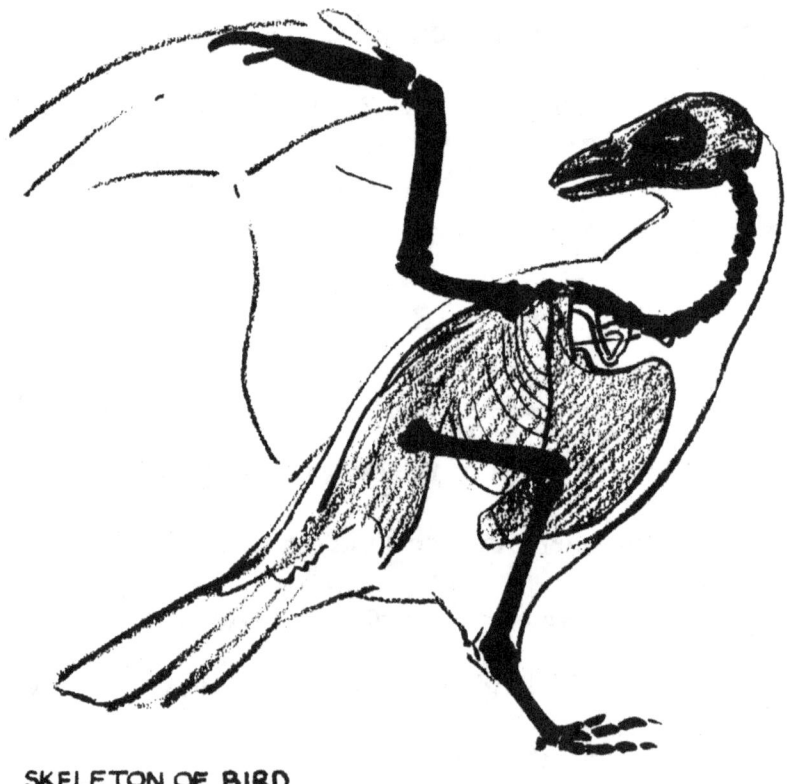

SKELETON OF BIRD

WINGS, FEATHERS AND FLIGHT

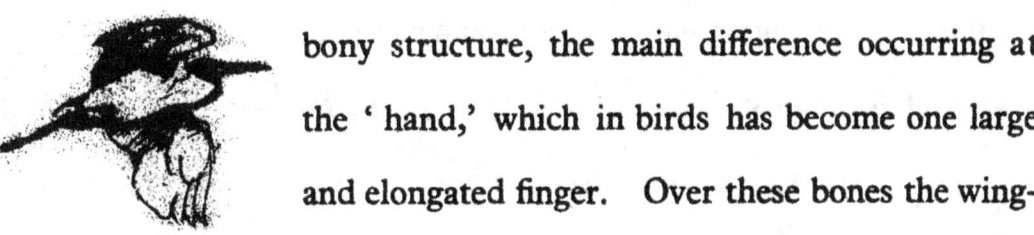

The wing of a bird is just like the arm of a man as regards its bony structure, the main difference occurring at the ' hand,' which in birds has become one large and elongated finger. Over these bones the wing-muscles and feathers are placed in such a way as to form what is known as the camber of a bird's wing. You will realise this when looking along a bird's open wing, as in the little sketch of a heron flying, it will be seen to curve upwards, umbrella fashion. If you push an open umbrella up and down quickly you will find it much easier to push it up than down because the camber of the umbrella seems to grip the air on the downward pull. This is roughly the principle that enables a bird to fly.

On page 21 is a view of a bird's wing as seen from above. The feathers are grouped in clearly defined masses. Into the long finger or " hand " of the bird are fitted the first flight feathers or primaries, usually 10 in number. From the forearm grow the secondary flight feathers, usually about 12 or 14 in number. The other groups serve to streamline the wing, build up its camber and give support to the flight feathers. The underside of the wing is supported in the same manner. At the junction of the wing and shoulder are a clearly marked group of feathers called the scapular. These feathers in most birds are quite large and besides streamlining the lines of the wing to the body they also cover the junction of wing and body when the wing is folded in the resting bird, preventing moisture from trickling down inside. The diagram shows you how these groups arrange themselves when the wing is folded.

This arrangement of feathers is the same in all birds, although the relative proportions of the various groups may differ. You will see from my diagrams that the feathers overlap each other and all point one way. They act like the tiles of a roof for draining water off. You will see in the drawing of a feather that the quill or central rib is *not* in the middle. This is because this particular feather is a flight feather and it is only the flight feathers which have the quill in this position. In the overlapping of the feathers, the broad edge is underneath so that a wing looked at from above shows only the narrow

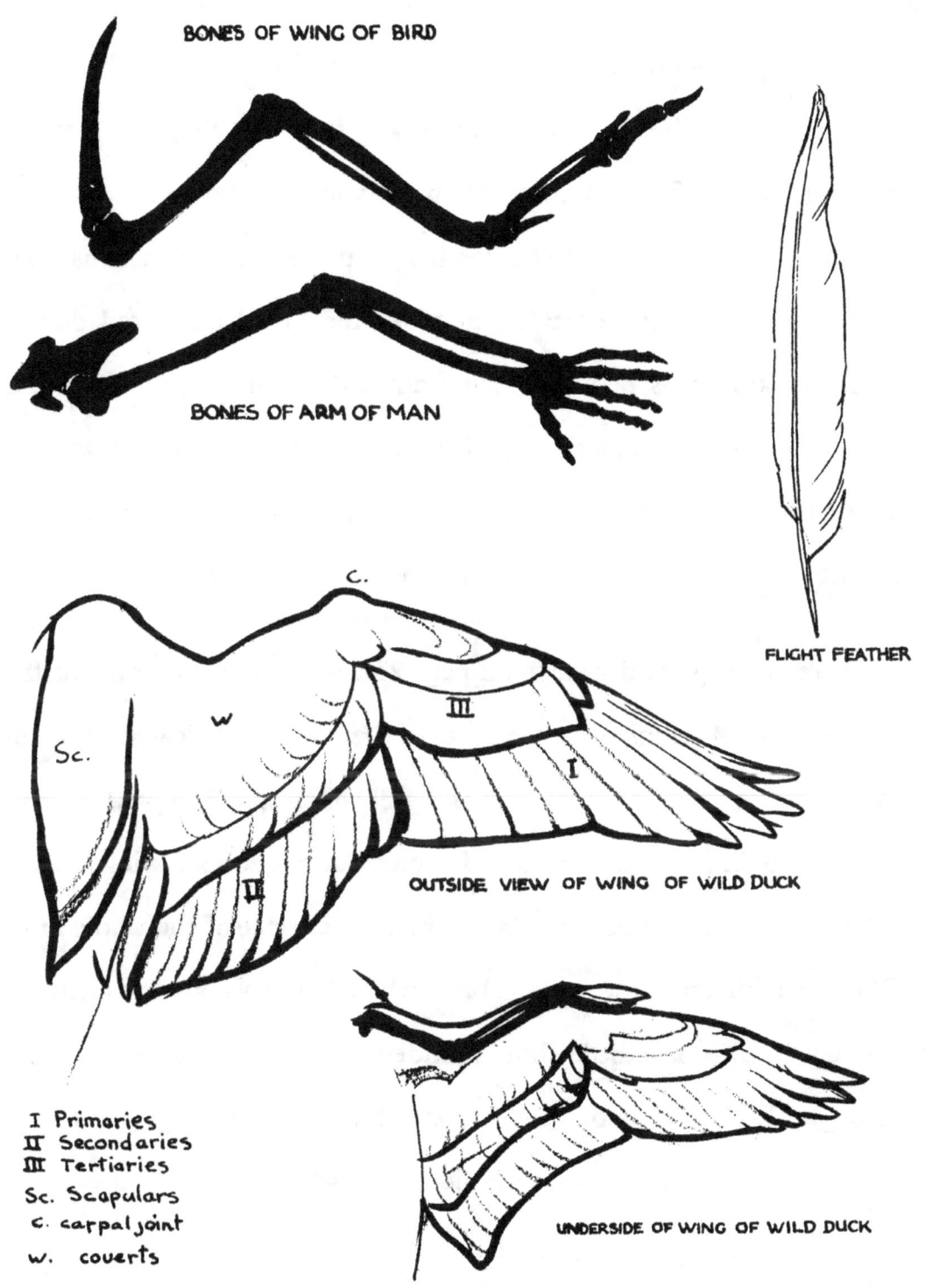

BONES OF WING OF BIRD

BONES OF ARM OF MAN

FLIGHT FEATHER

OUTSIDE VIEW OF WING OF WILD DUCK

UNDERSIDE OF WING OF WILD DUCK

I Primaries
II Secondaries
III Tertiaries
Sc. Scapulars
c. carpal joint
w. couerts

or ' leading ' edge of the feather and from beneath only the broad or trailing edge. This is a very important thing to remember when drawing birds in flight, because when the wings are pressed down, the " trailing " broad edge of the feather is pushed tightly against the next feather. On the upstroke however the broad ends trail downwards, making gaps between each feather through which the air can pass : it is by the power of resistance to the air of the downward stroke that a bird can haul itself up into the sky. The drawings of a heron and a gull flying show this principle at work.

There is a page of drawings on page 23 which show you some of the various types of wings there are, in all of them I have indicated the main masses of the feathers. The first is a gull which spends a great part of its life in gliding and has developed a long, narrow pointed wing for this purpose. Notice the perfect streamlined appearance of the whole bird. Of quite a different order are the birds which live in woods and enclosed country : they have little short rounded wings to enable them to fly through close-cover with ease. Some, like the blackbird, have long tails to enable them to make rapid turns whilst flying at speed.

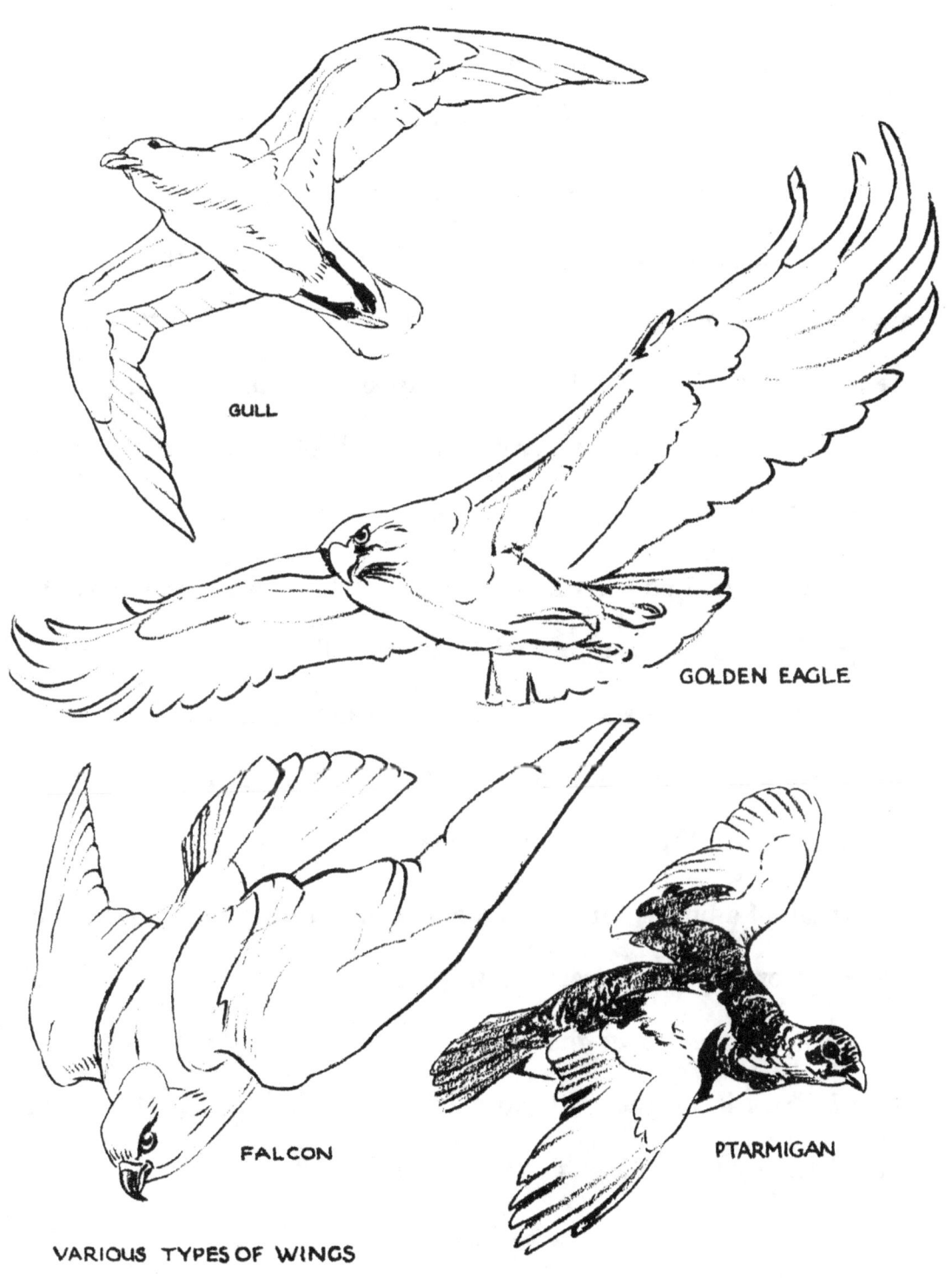

GULL

GOLDEN EAGLE

FALCON

PTARMIGAN

VARIOUS TYPES OF WINGS

Game birds and others of the open moorland where straight flying is all that is required have short, rounded tails.

You will recognise the big bird in the middle as an eagle. Look at its great wing-span—notice how the ends of its flight feathers are cut away towards the tip—they look rather like fingers when the bird is seen soaring in the sky. In varying proportions this type of wing is seen on buzzards, herons and crows. Ducks display them on the downward thrust of their wings during their first jump off from the water.

It is the falcons and hawks who combine the most perfect streamlining with the greatest muscular power. Their powerful muscles give them the heavy-shouldered look of the true athlete, and drive narrow pinions with such force and rapidity that they can easily overhaul most other birds on the wing.

The tail of a bird is formed in a fan of overlapping feathers, usually about 12 or 14. The main thing to remember is that the central feather is on the *top* of the tail, the others overlapping each other from *beneath* it on each side, so that when the tail is closed it is the central feather you see, with the edges of the others receding beneath.

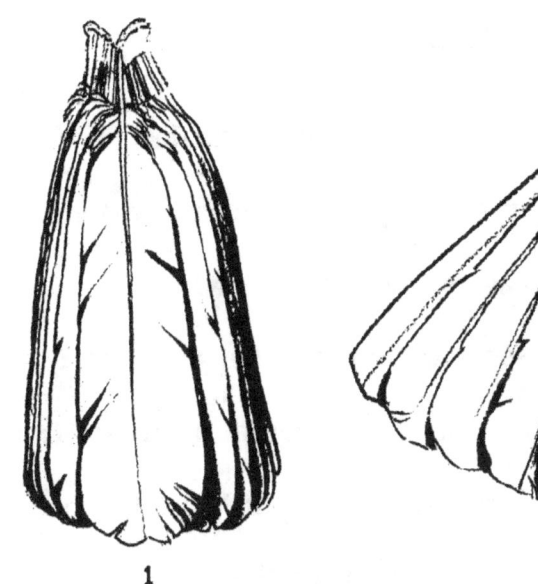

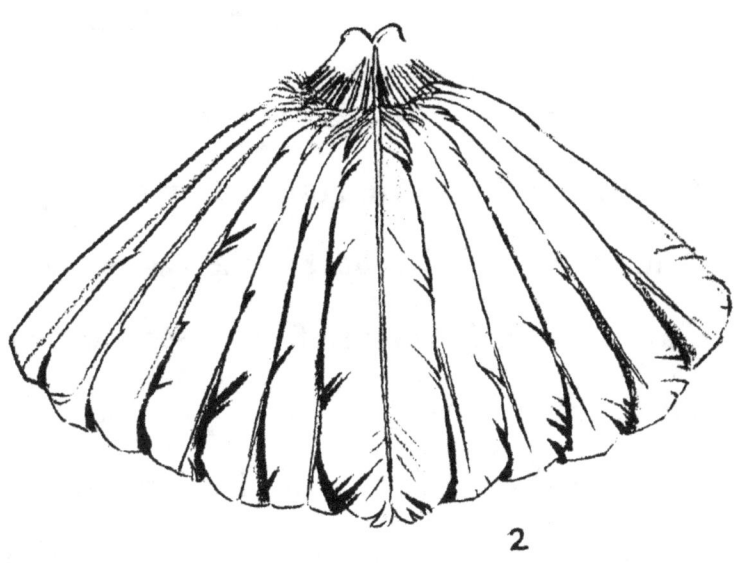

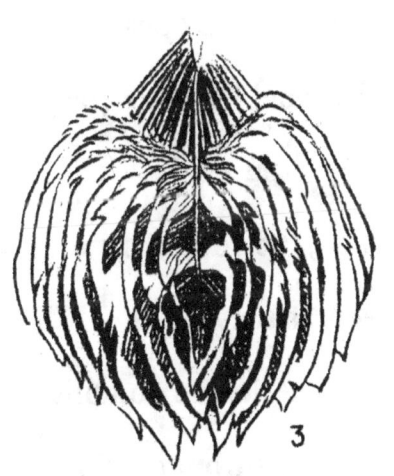

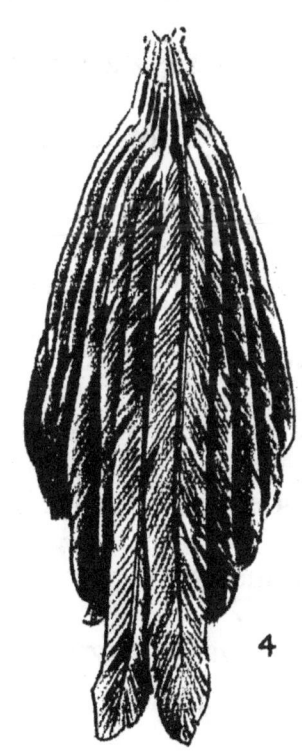

1 WOODPIGEON --(closed)
2 WOODPIGEON---(open)
3 FEMALE WILD DUCK
4 MAGPIE

BEAKS

I have drawn on page 27 some of the various types of beaks. These differences in shape are governed by the way they find and eat their food. Some are like hooks—the eagles and hawks—who use their beaks to tear and rend their food. Some are long and dagger-shaped—like the herons who spear fish and eels on it. Different again are the long probe-like beaks of some of the waders. These they use to probe the soft mud of the estuaries where they search for their food.

Curlew, oyster-catchers, snipe and woodcock come under this category. The woodcock has a very interesting adaptation. It possesses a very sensitive, movable tip to its long bill, which enables it to grasp a worm under the mud, and withdraw it with very little effort.

Swallows and swifts possess short beaks which, however, have a mouth of great width to enable them to catch insects as they fly.

A duck possesses a very special sort of beak. The inside contains rows of small plates, like teeth which act as sieves, through which water is strained, the small particles of food being retained. These are just a few of the various types, there are many more.

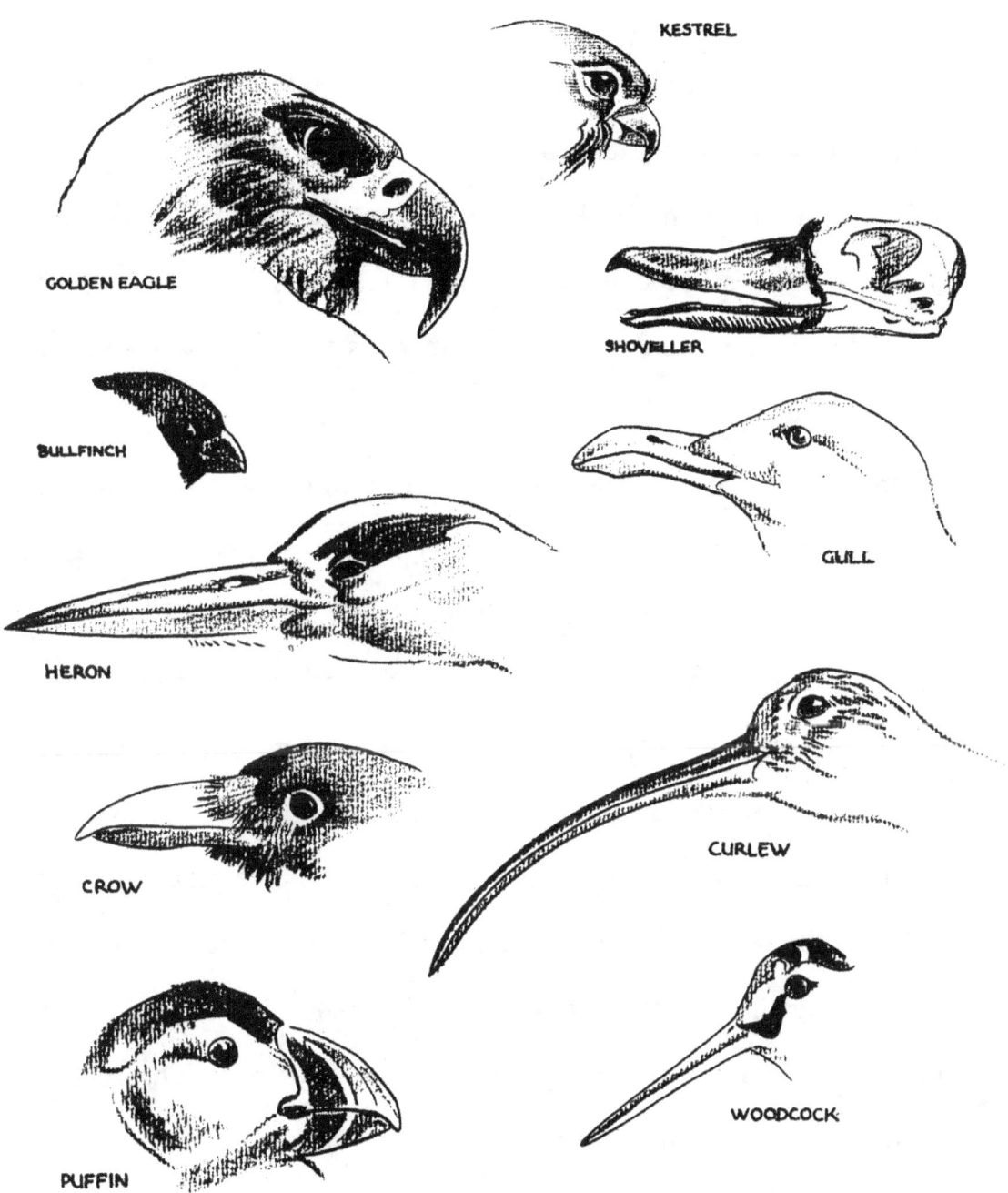

KESTREL

GOLDEN EAGLE

SHOVELLER

BULLFINCH

GULL

HERON

CROW

CURLEW

PUFFIN

WOODCOCK

FEET

The scales of a bird's foot are most beautifully patterned, being arranged in a very decorative way. The first toe which corresponds to our thumb, is at the back, the second on the inside and has two bones, the third is in the middle and has three joints, the fourth on the outside has four joints. This arrangement is the rule in practically every sort of bird.

Opposite are various types of feet. The birds which perch, you will notice, have a long thumb or hind-toe in order to grasp the bough. These birds hop on the ground. Eagles and hawks have it strongly developed in order to grasp their prey and consequently have a very free movement. In ducks, and most birds who spend the best part of their time on the water, the three toes are joined by a web and the hind-toe is barely seen at all. In the swallow, which spends the greater part of its life on the wing, the feet are used mainly for clinging so all four toes are together. Woodpeckers and cuckoos are different : they have their toes in pairs, two in front and two behind. The cuckoo can transfer its second toe to the back or front as it pleases.

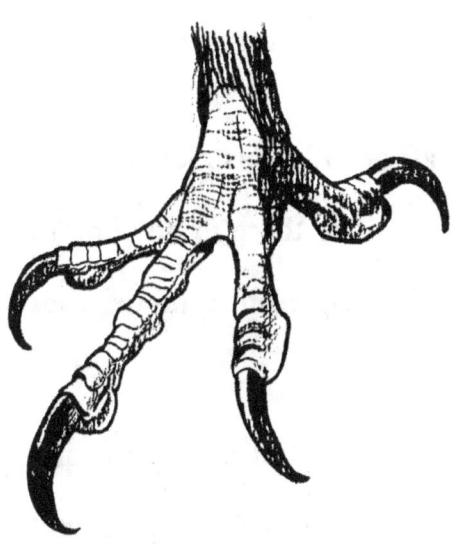

GOLDEN EAGLE
(EXTENDED)

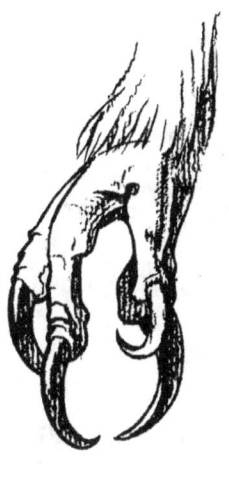

GOLDEN EAGLE
(CLOSED)

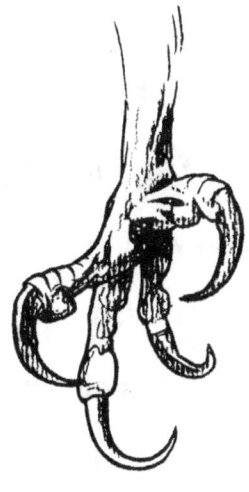

OSPREY

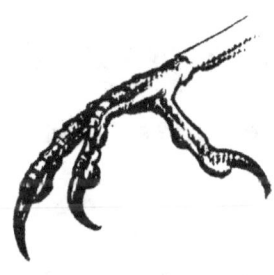

ROOK

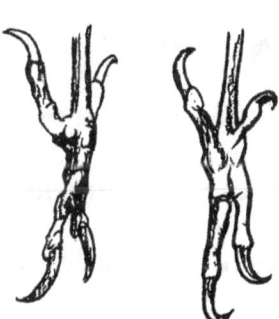

WOODPECKER
(ZYGODACTYLE)

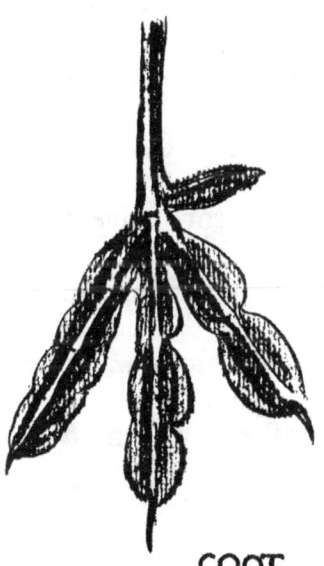

COOT

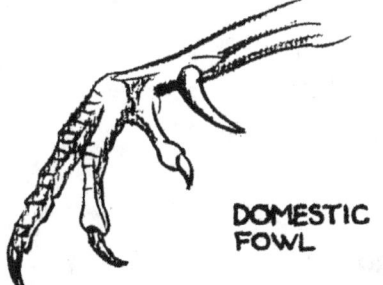

DOMESTIC
FOWL

DIFFERENT TYPES
OF FEET.

DUCKS

Draw with long sure lines. Do not be afraid of a mistake, you can always start again if things go wrong, and besides there is no time to waste in making tentative scratches when drawing from a model that may fly away any minute!

The Drawing of the standing duck "A" is executed mostly in long sweeping curves indicating the direction and area of the principal shapes. Curved lines always suggest movement and rhythm—but the basic construction and squareness of the bird should not be overlooked. Diagram " B " shows where this squareness may be looked for as a corrective to any tendency to over-emphasize the curves. Such over-emphasis always makes the drawing look weak and lacking in construction. The little drawing of the head shows how the position of the eye can always be determined by its relation to the oval shape of the cheek.

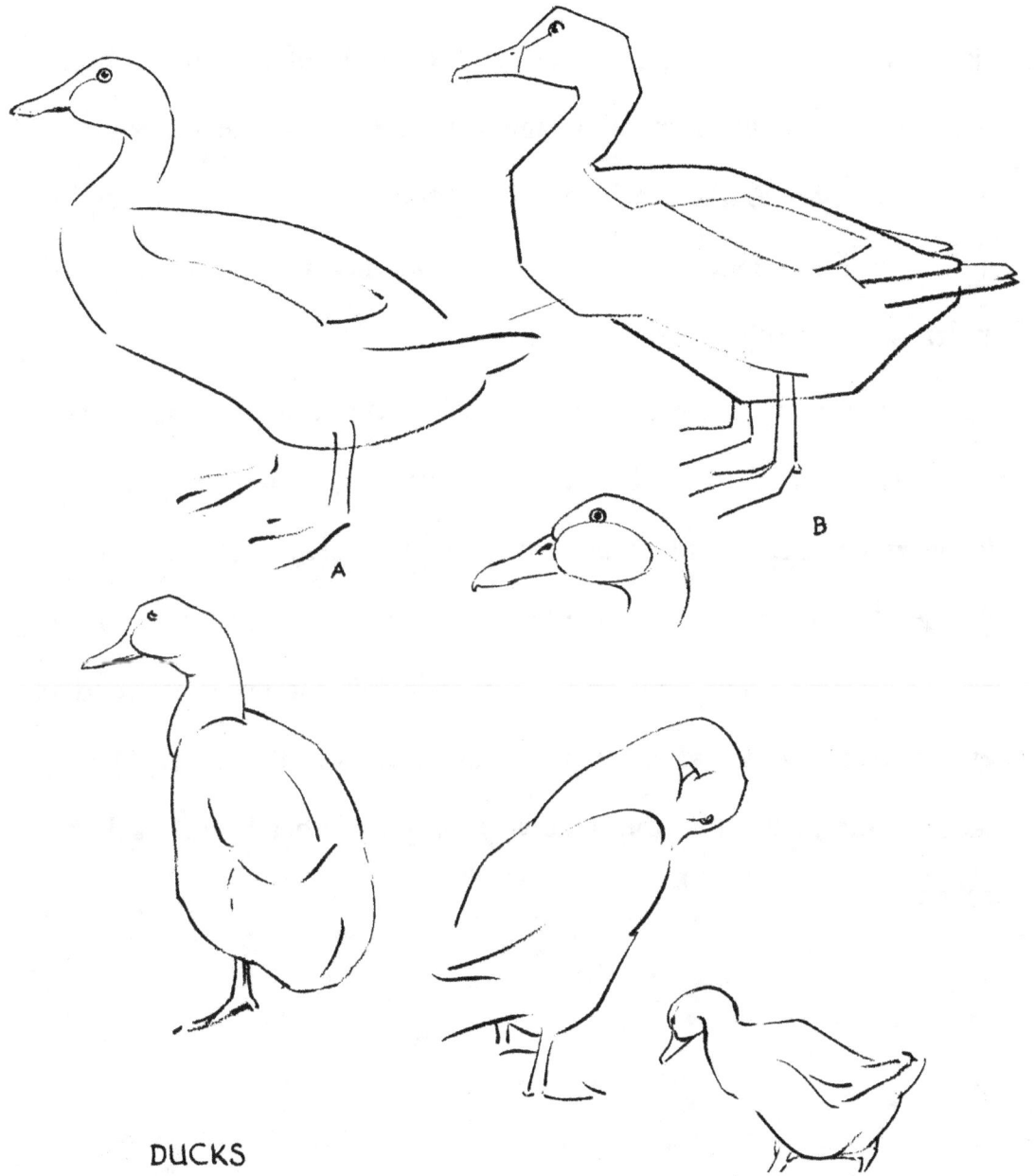

A

B

DUCKS

DUCKS, IN THE WATER

A duck's body is built like a boat, to float, and if you remember this you can't go far wrong. Careful observation of the way its breast pushes the water in front of it, and the position of the waterline, is very necessary. Make the bird float *in* the water and not merely sit *on* it. Willing models can easily be obtained on every park-lake by arming yourself with breadcrumbs.

There are many different species of wild duck but perhaps the best known is the Mallard. The drake looks very handsome with his glossy green head and neck, white collar, grey back and black upcurled tail coverts. His mate looks quite drab in comparison in her dress of mottled brown and buff. But then this sombre dress renders her nearly invisible when sitting motionless on the nest. Young males are marked in just the same way, only their heads and backs are darker.

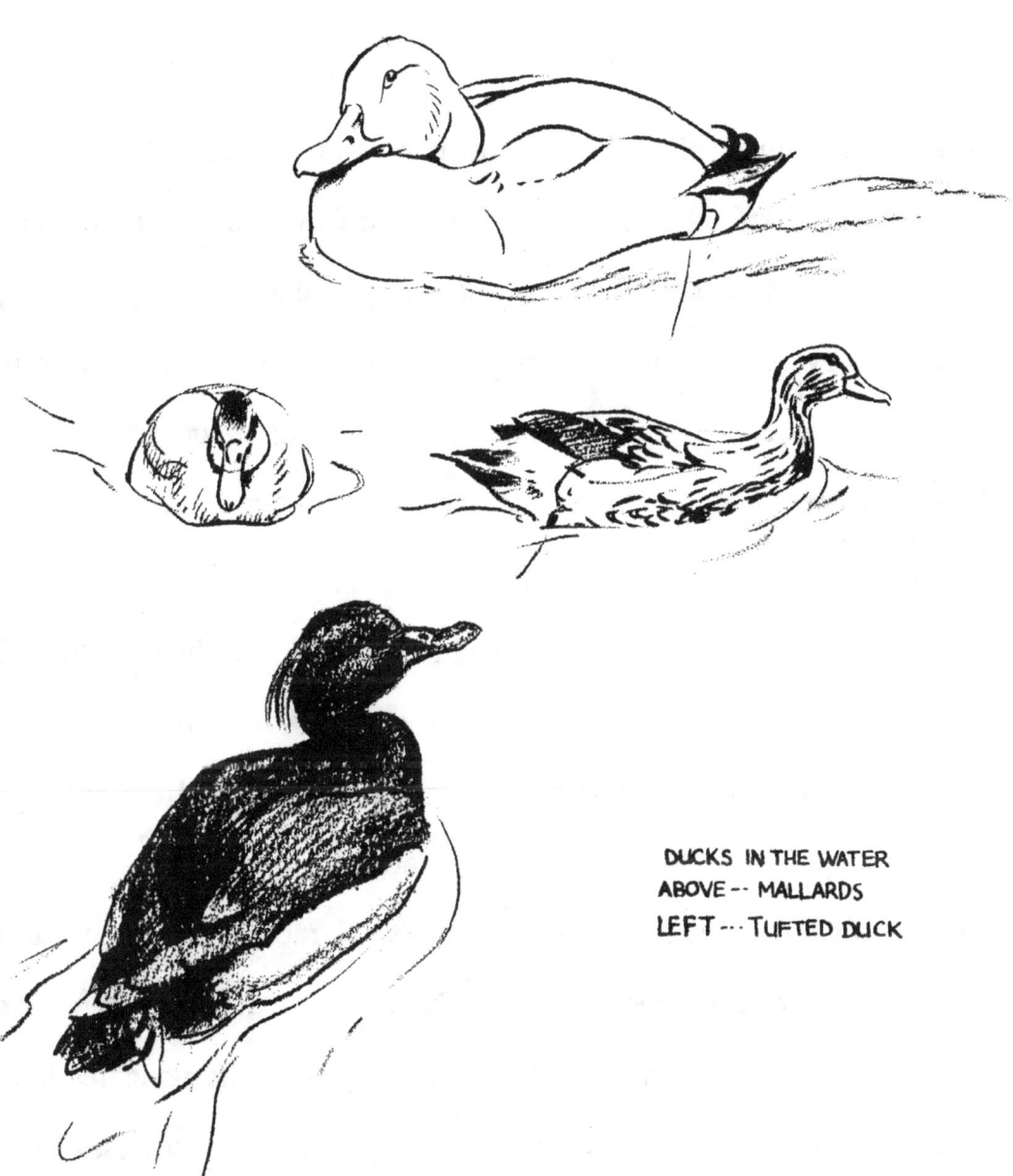

DUCKS IN THE WATER
ABOVE -- MALLARDS
LEFT --- TUFTED DUCK

WELL KNOWN BIRDS SEEN FROM THE BREAKFAST TABLE

Perhaps the most difficult of all birds to draw are those lively little birds which visit the bird-bath and breakfast tray in our own gardens. Their rapid movements, a constant source of delight to the onlooker, make it very difficult for the beginner to sketch them. So it is perhaps better to attempt drawing these birds after you have had a little practice drawing from the stately swan and quieter more reposeful duck.

On the opposite page is an apparently detailed study of a Missel thrush. But the two little diagrams above it show you how simple it is in its essentials. I looked first for the position and direction of the egg-shaped mass of its body—its relation to the bough—then the direction of the tail and position of head were rapidly indicated—and most important of all, the body must balance properly on legs whose feet grip the bough firmly. The main masses of the wing feathers were next observed, and then, to all intents and purposes, the important part of the drawing was done, the rest was simply a careful

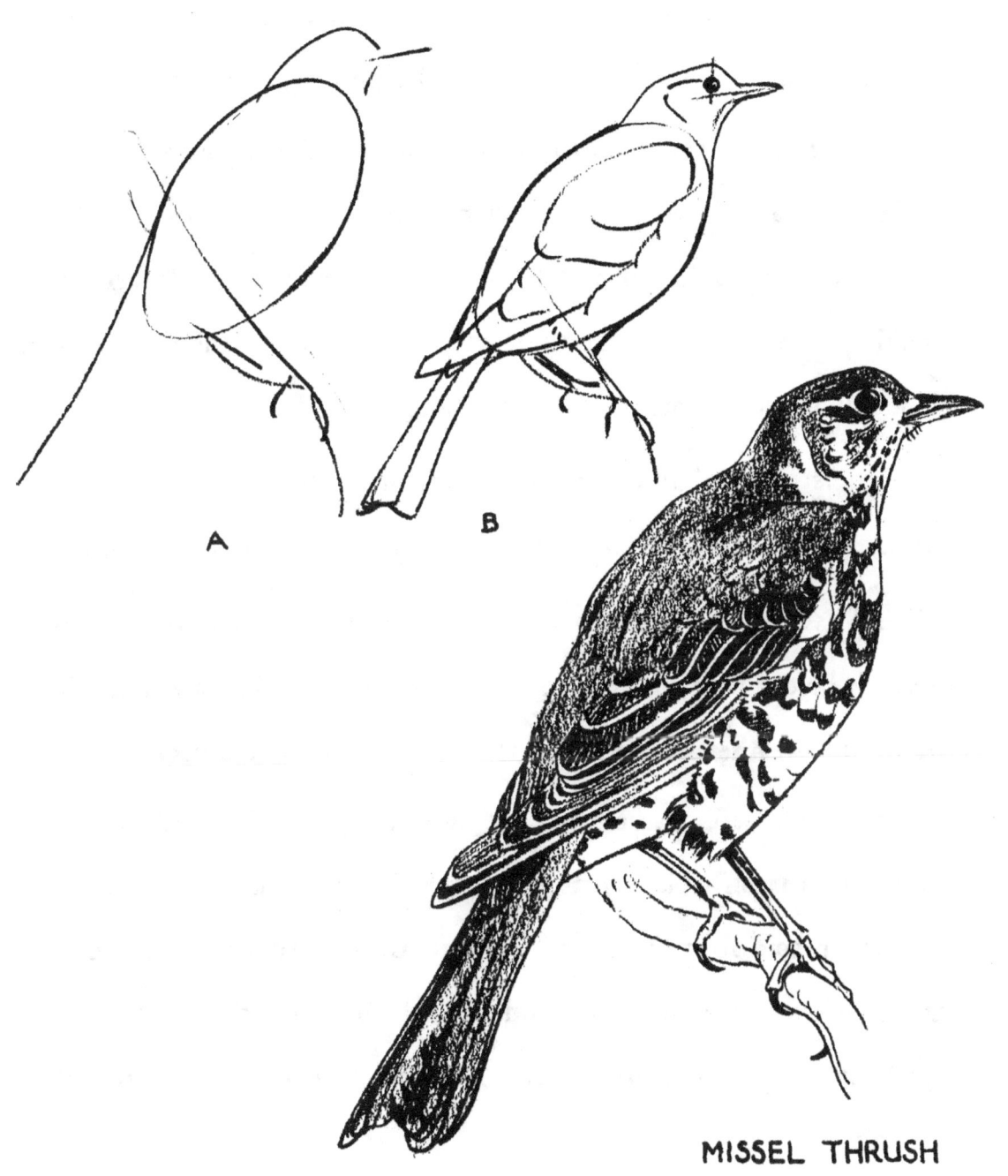

A

B

MISSEL THRUSH

study of the markings, and shading was used only to indicate the differences of light and dark colour in the plumage pattern.

These rapid sketches of thrushes were all done by the same method of observing and drawing the big shapes first with simple long lines—with a mere indication of pattern where it is thought such markings would be useful. These are the sort of drawings you should try for (I hope you will be more successful though !).

Speed is essential to catch such momentary poses as that of the cheeky thrush, standing on tiptoe, who watched me as I drew him !

The Missel thrush is the largest British thrush—the spotting on its breast is bolder than that of the song thrush. Its habit of singing in the wildest weather has earned it the name of the Storm-cock.

The bottom left of the page are two studies of the Redwing—a continental thrush which visits us in the winter and is particularly in evidence in cold frosty weather. The remaining studies are of song-thrushes—excepting for the outline sketch of a blackbird—(bottom right) instantly recognisable from a starling by his long tail and jet uniform and orange bill.

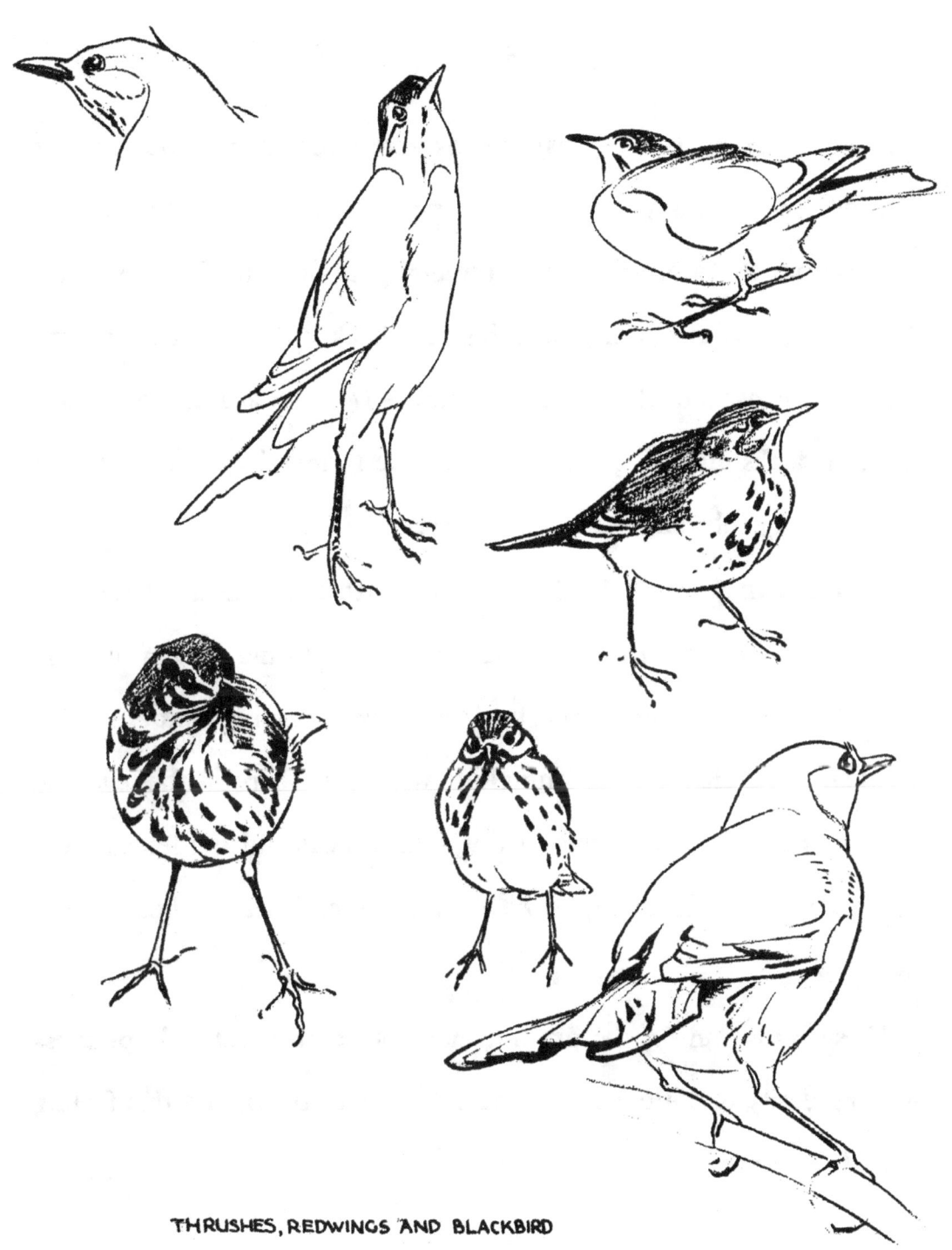

THRUSHES, REDWINGS AND BLACKBIRD

STARLINGS

A most amazing bird—always racing across the lawn at top-speed in an endeavour to satisfy an insatiable appetite. In his off-duty moments he may sometimes be seen on a chimney pot, with the feathers of his throat loosened and spiky, opening his beak and indulging in any song but his own, for he is a great mimic—(A.). Starlings congregate in huge flocks and do great service to the farmer by their wholesale slaughter of grubs and other insect pests.

At sunset they return in their thousands to their ancestral roosting places. In London there are many such roosting places on old buildings, and familiar to the business man returning home is their peculiar " frizzling " song mingling with the roar of the evening traffic. The plumage of this bird is a most beautiful irridescent coat which gleams in the sunlight with ever-varying hues of shot purples and greens.

These birds run on the ground, not hop, and a general spikiness and angularity of outline seems characteristic of them, and this feeling should be apparent in the studies.

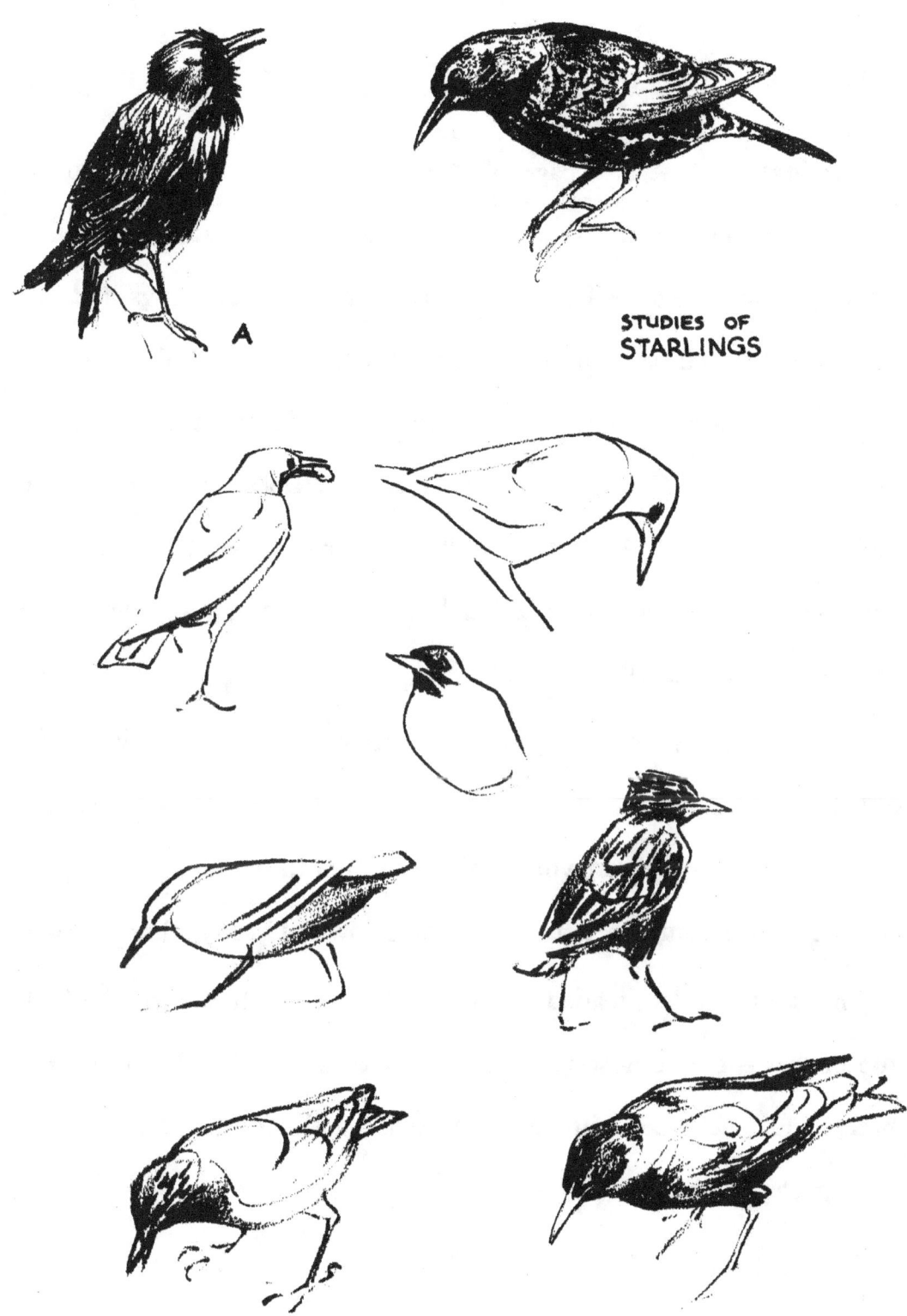

A

STUDIES OF
STARLINGS

BIRDS OF WOOD AND HEDGEROW

The first of these is a page of studies of the blackcap—which, as might be assumed from its name, is easily recognisable among warblers by its jet black head. The neck is ashen grey—back wings and tail an ashy-buff—chin white—legs and feet lead-coloured. It is a migrant and as a songster second only to the nightingale, it sings by night as well as by day, and its song is sometimes mistaken for the nightingale's. It is a delicately built little bird and in some of these studies its feathers are loosened and fluffed out, giving it a more rotund appearance than usual.

The next page is devoted to studies of the Nuthatch, who spends most of his time running up and down tree-trunks searching in the crevices of the bark for the insects on which he lives most of the summer. He seems just as much at home when hanging upside down as in any other position.

The squat bullet headed shape of the bullfinch is typical of all the finches—its strong squat beak for extracting seeds. Its bright red breast and black head with pale grey back—make it easily recognisable among the finches.

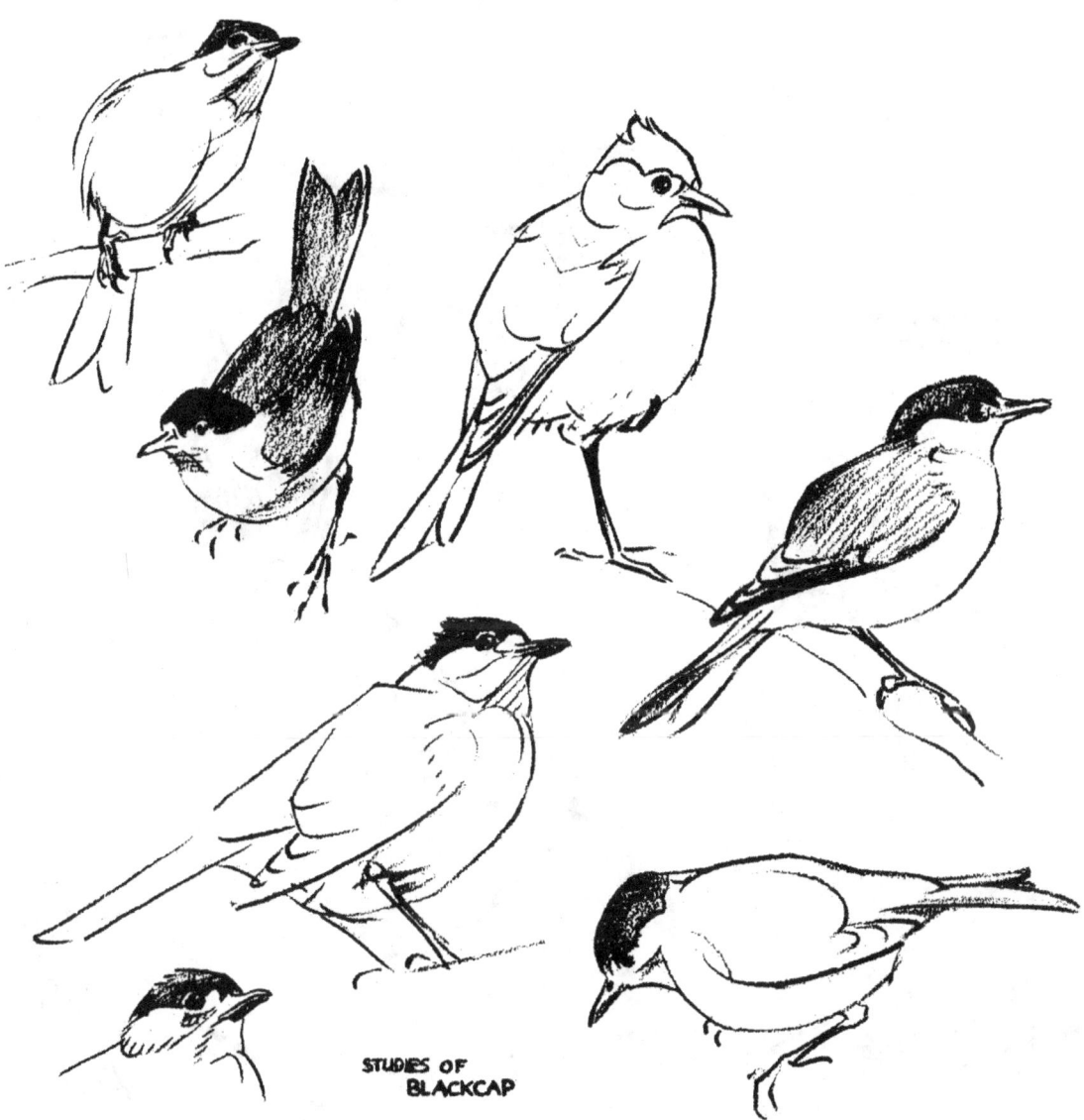

STUDIES OF
BLACKCAP

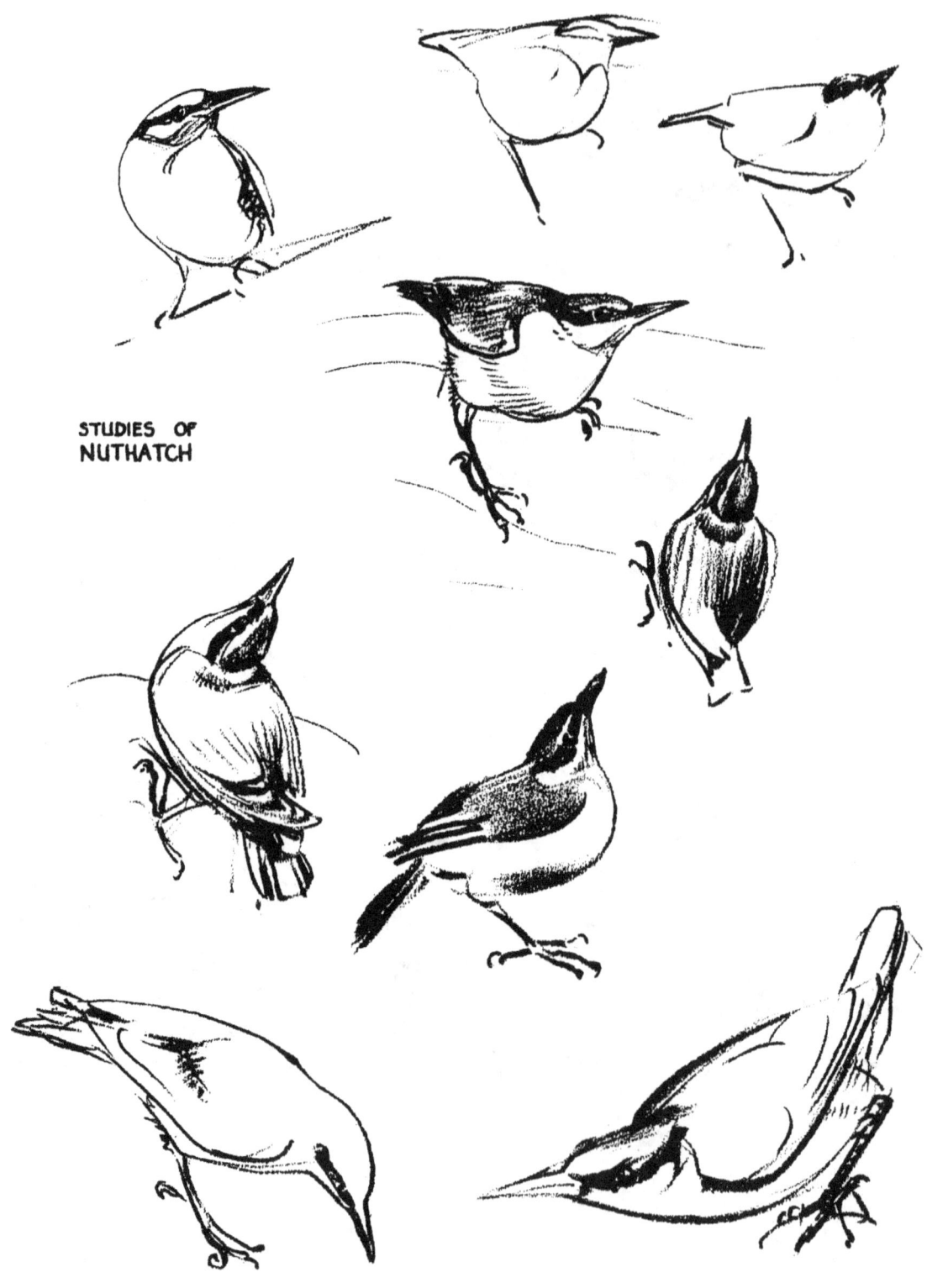

STUDIES OF
NUTHATCH

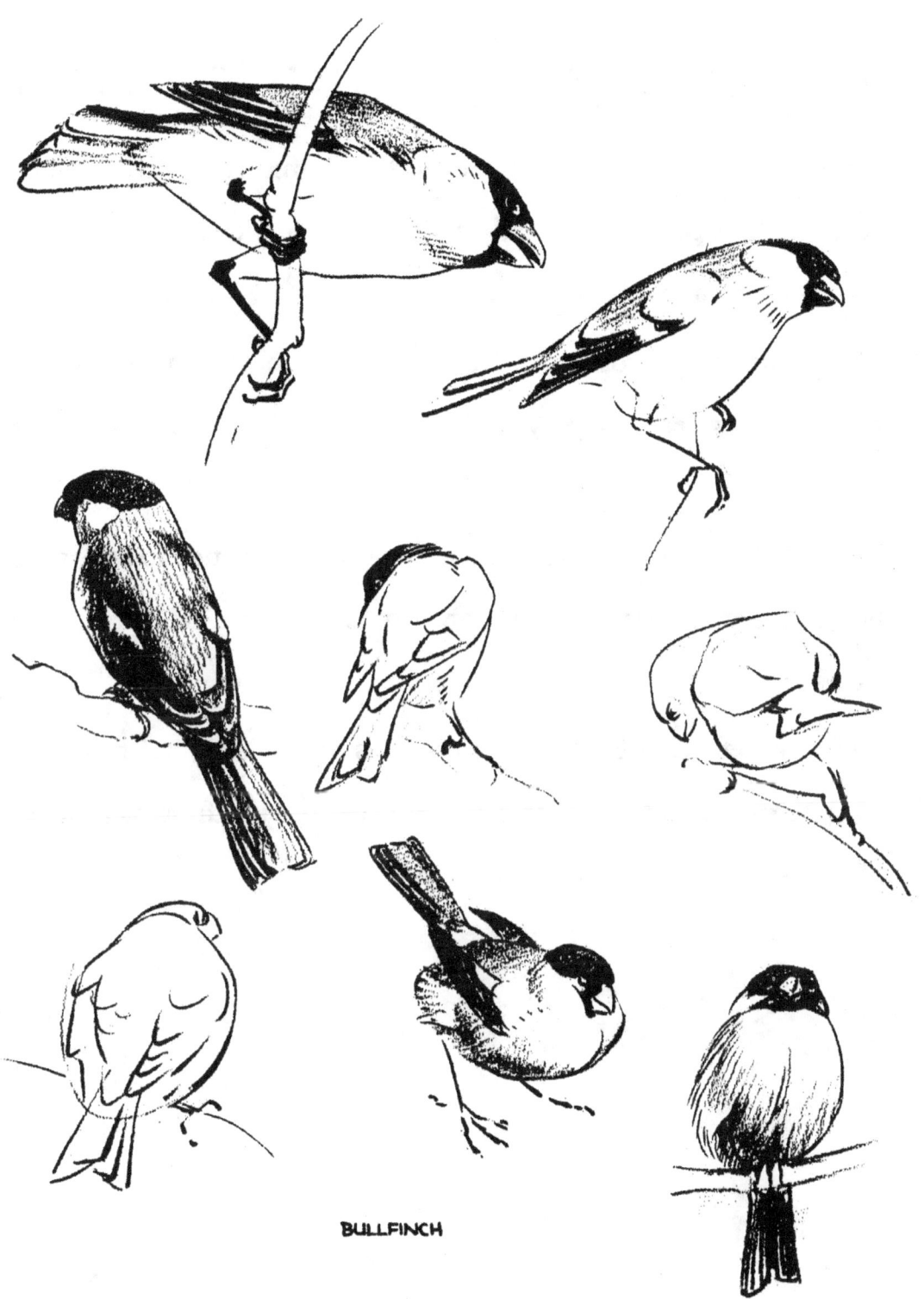

BULLFINCH

OYSTER-CATCHER AND CURLEW

The oyster-catcher is one of our most beautiful shore birds with its striking plumage of black and white simply divided into clear-cut masses—it is an excellent subject to draw.

When drawing birds at rest, balanced on one foot, note how the supporting leg leans slightly inward to preserve the balance of the bird.

The birds in the sketch are resting, waiting for the tide to fall, when they will wander over the ooze and rocks in search of cockles and worms.

The top left hand bird is a curlew. Its long curved bill may vary in length from four to seven inches. It takes its name from its peculiar wild cry—familiar on shore and estuary.

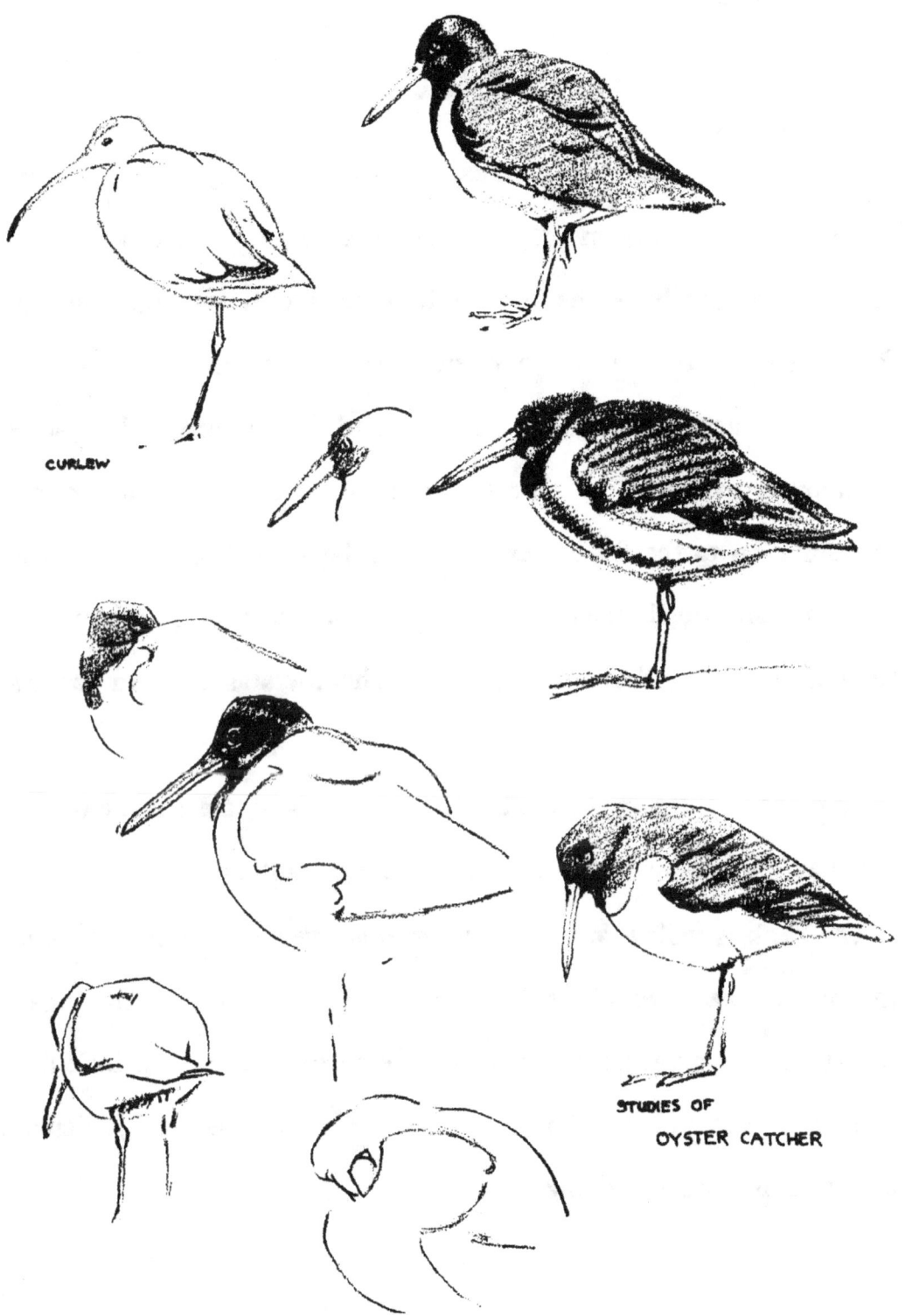

CURLEW

STUDIES OF
OYSTER CATCHER

HERON

This most graceful bird, is an expert fisher, and may be seen wading along the banks of stream or lake. He hurls his beak like a spear at his victim, and transfixes the fish. Often he stands still on one leg, for his characteristic attitude when at rest, with his head drawn in between hunched shoulders. These birds offer great decorative possibilities to the artist. Birds of this type were a constant source of inspiration to the far-Eastern artists of Japan and China. On the wing they are equally magnificent, rising slowly with long legs trailing, the head gradually drawn back into the shoulders as the bird gathers speed and rises.

Its flight feathers are black, but only the ends of these show in the sketches, protruding from beneath its grey mantle.

The beak is yellow and the legs greenish yellow. When drawing the outstretched neck, look for angularity at the bend rather than curvature—too great an insistance on the curve will make it look like a piece of bent tubing. The bony structure is inferred in a judicious use of straight lines and angles.

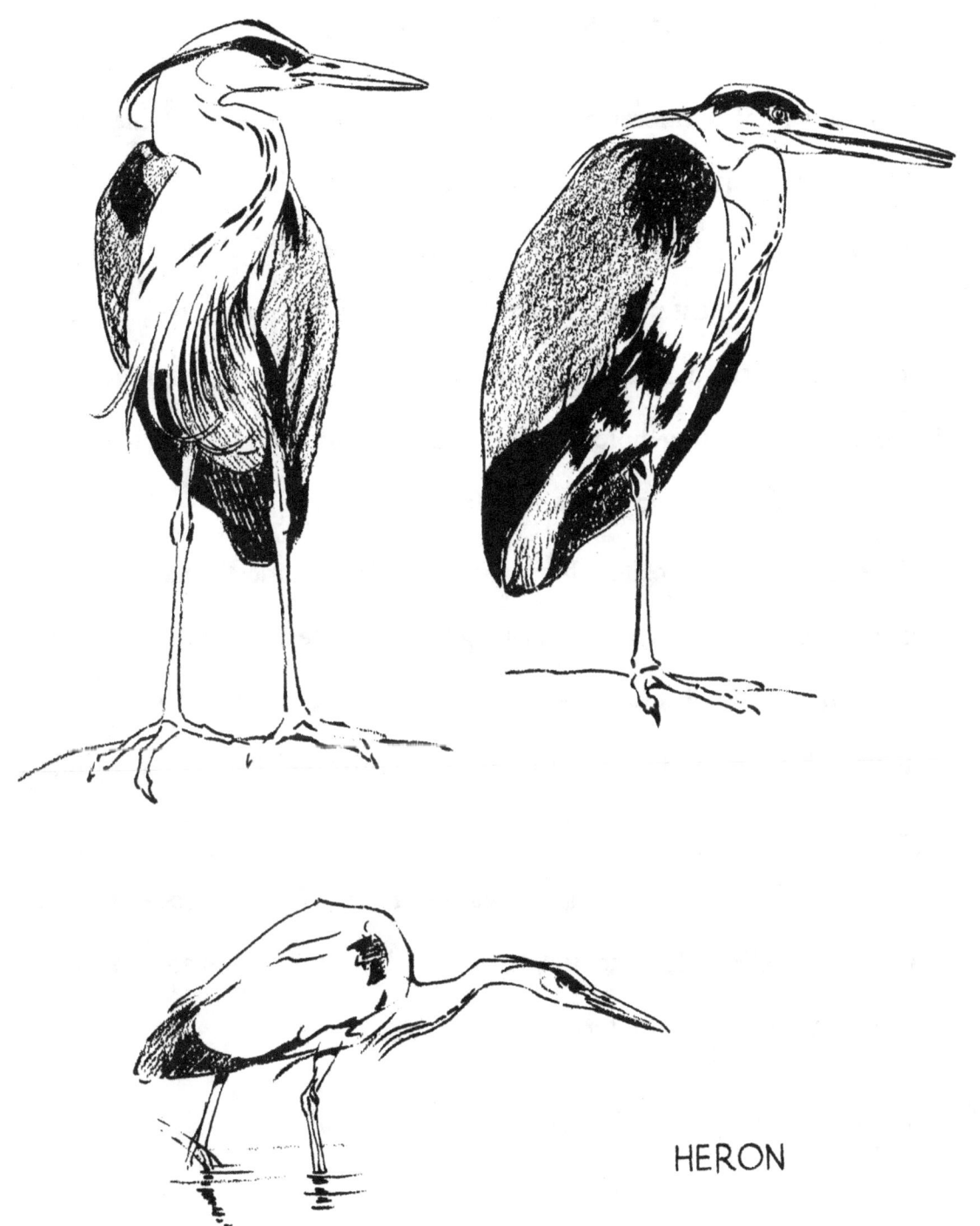

HERON

KINGFISHER

To the casual wanderer along the shores of a stream the Kingfisher is generally a darting flash of blue as the bird dashes for the shelter of the bank. This bird however, is more common than is usually thought, its favourite resorts being rivers and streams which have stretches of perpendicular clay banks. These banks are necessary for the location of its nesting-hole—a tunnel driven into the face of the clay to a depth of about two and a half feet.

The sketches opposite show the bird in its most characteristic position seated on a branch overhanging the water, into which it will plunge in pursuit of small fry and minnows. It is a very beautifully coloured bird with its unmatched, brilliant-blue back and rufous breast.

Its eye has a cold and fishy gleam—and its feathers indeed look rather like scales. It is to the smaller fish what the heron is to the larger trout and eels—a terror !

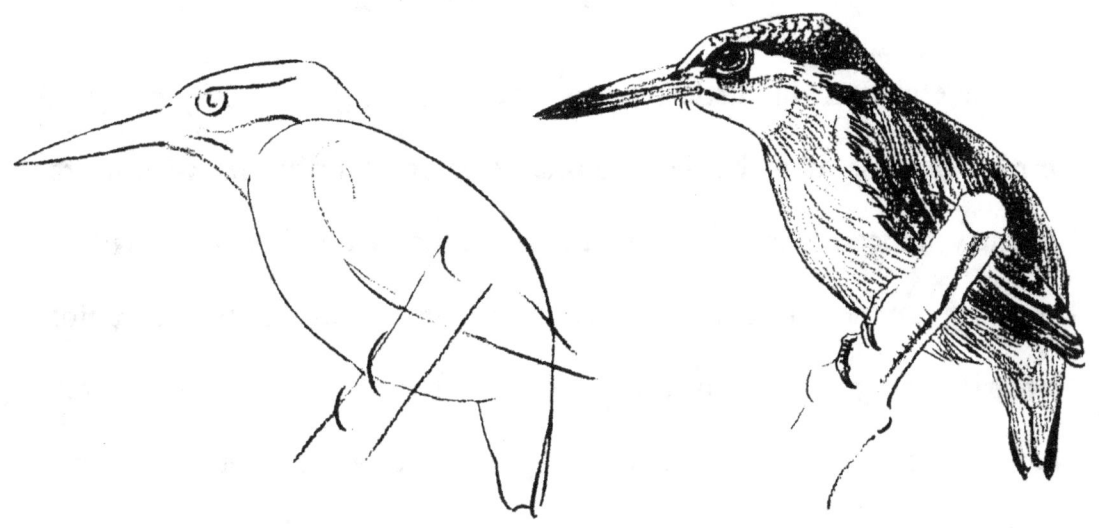

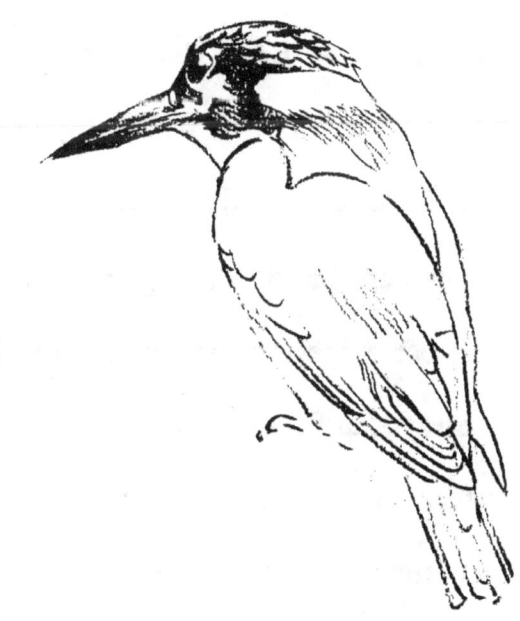

KINGFISHER

PARTRIDGE

I have chosen this little bird to represent the great family of ' game birds ' because it is by far the one most commonly met with in the country, indeed most of us must at one time or another, have had our country rambles suddenly startled by its abrupt departure on rapidly whirring wings, from our very feet.   In five of these studies the bird had so puffed out its feathers as to give it almost the appearance of a feathered football.   It was basking in the sun on a bright frosty day.

You will notice that in some of these studies I have utilized light and shade in order to obtain a greater appearance of solidity.   The rule is—light comes forward and dark retires—put any sphere, an orange, for instance, on the table in front of you—and you can learn all the principles of light and shade from it.

The bottom right hand drawing shows the bird with feathers pressed down.   The partridge is a beautifully marked bird, with dark rufous stripes on breast-feathers.   The light quills of its wing coverts make a clear pattern of pale flicks against the dark mottling of the back.

The head study is of a red-legged partridge.

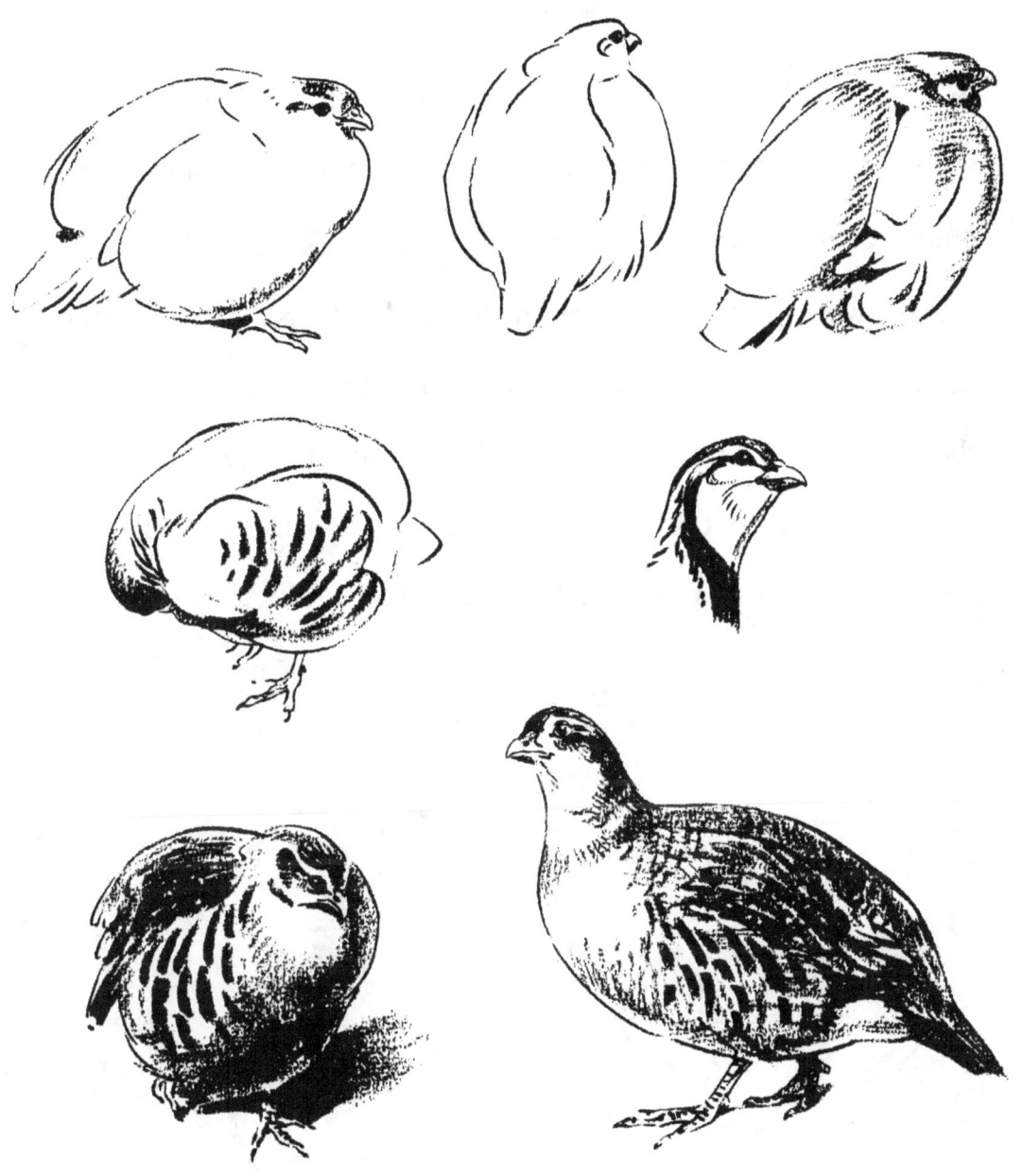

PARTRIDGE

DOMESTIC FOWL

Although not a British Bird in the strict sense of the word, the domestic fowl is such a typical part of the farm and countryside.

Points to notice are the wedge-like shape of the masses, particularly the hen—which is not a very beautiful bird, unless one searches very carefully for the main lines and rhythm which follow through her rather ungainly bulk. The Cockerel, however, is a very lordly bird, and in the hands of the artist is full of great decorative possibilities, particularly in the curve of the sickle feathers which hang over the real tail.

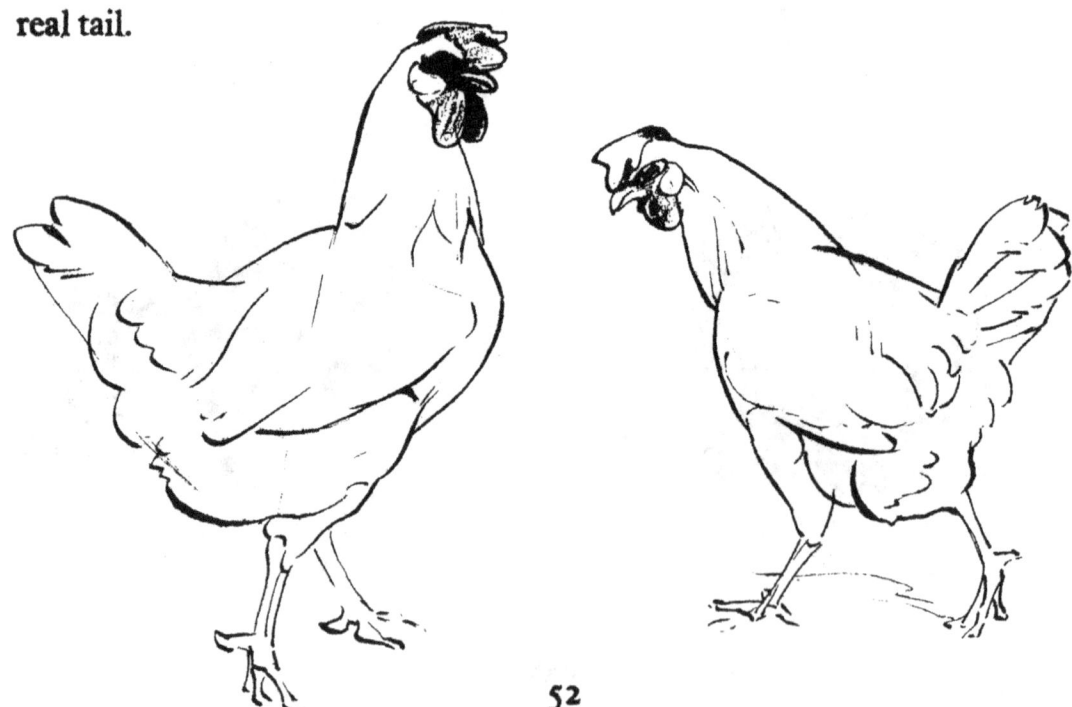

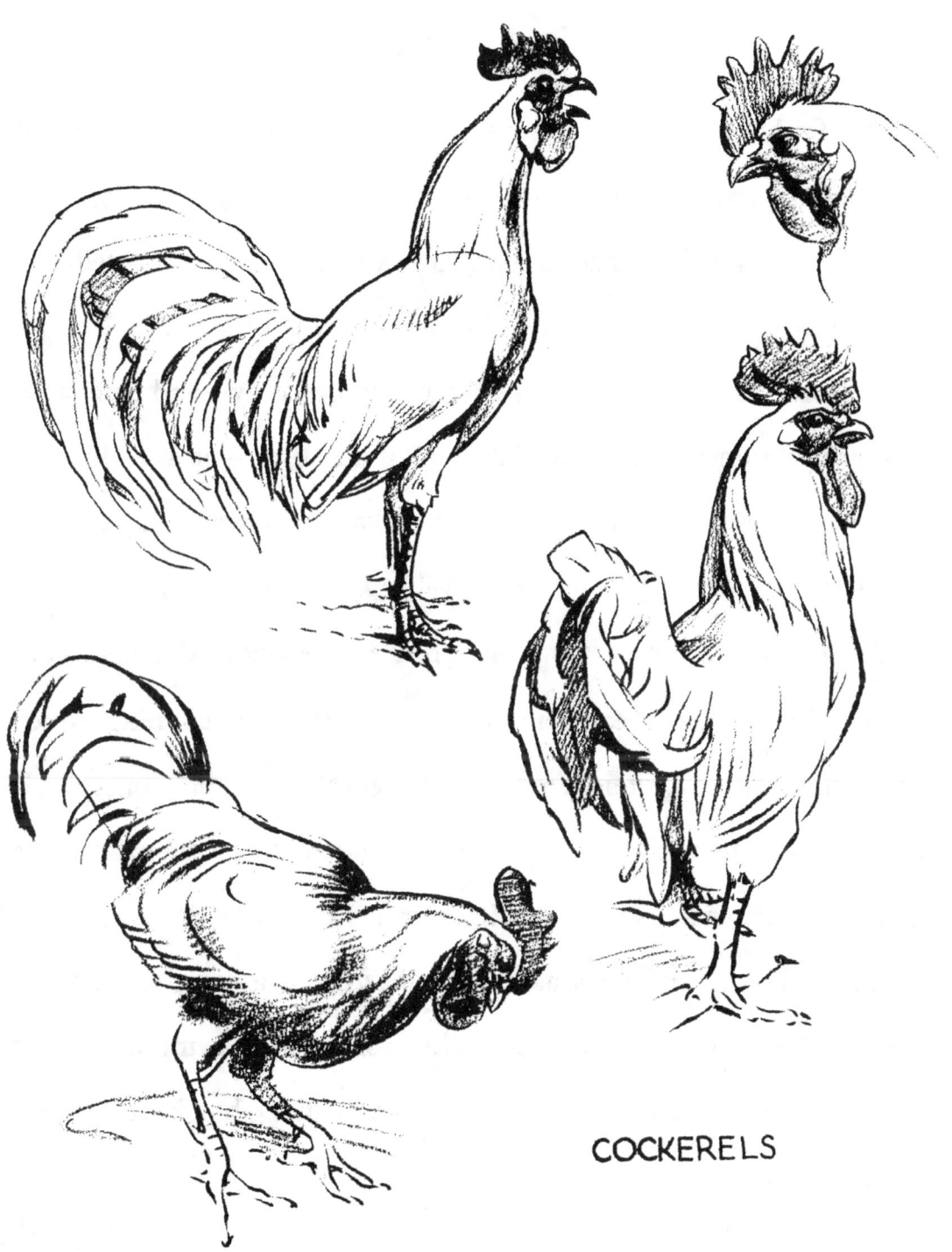

COCKERELS

RAVEN

This fairly rare bird, is however first in popular imagination of the crow family, and I suppose is responsible for more legends than most birds. It does in fact stand first among its kind, being more intelligent and highly developed than any other of our birds.

Its remarkable eyesight can spot carrion miles away—and its equally remarkable stomach seems to digest anything dead,—or alive for that matter—which falls beneath this great pickaxe of a beak. The colour is really a wonderfully ' shot ' purply-black, which glistens in the sun.

To the artist and naturalist it is a bird full of interesting character. An ageless wisdom gleams in its cunning eye : a cunning which however seems to be tempered with a roguish sense of humour. It is remarkable that in the face of such relentless persecution from the hands of man, such a large bird has escaped complete extinction.

A straight and rugged squareness indicative of a compact strength are the characteristic lines to be looked for when drawing the sitting bird. On the wing it appears to be a heavy flier—but in reality is a superb master of wing-craft.

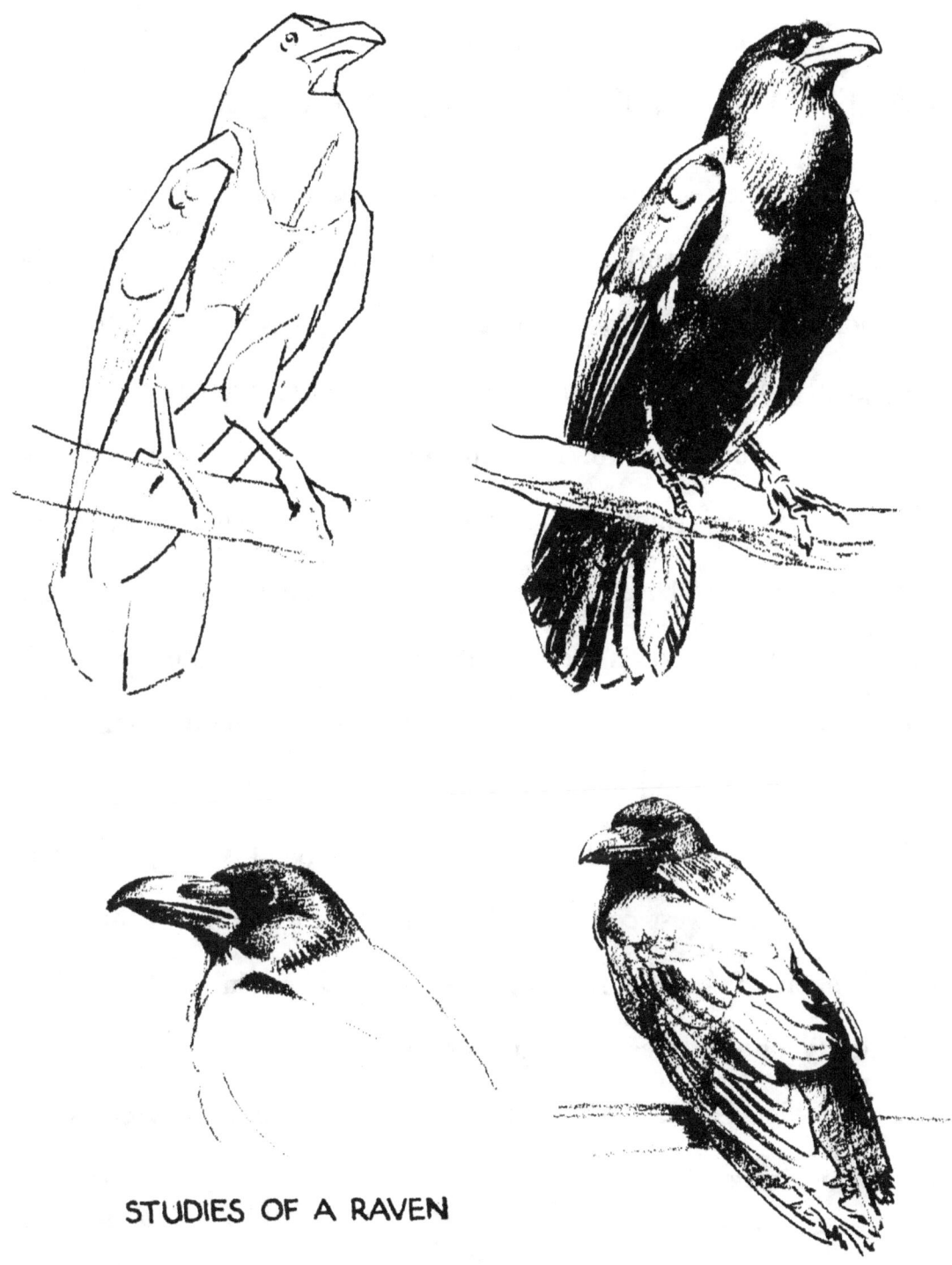

STUDIES OF A RAVEN

THREE BIRDS OF PREY
BARN OWL, BUZZARD AND GOLDEN EAGLE

The Owl, like the Raven, is a bird which has been immortalized by the literature of the world. These drawings are of a Barn Owl, a fairly common bird but owing to its dislike of sunlight is rarely seen. Note the arrangement of the feathers, forming the facial disc round the eyes, so typical of these birds. Their round heads have a startling flexibility and they can turn their heads right round and look straight at you over their backs.

In these studies I have not attempted to delineate plumage markings, but have concentrated on the beautiful simple forms of the bird itself. I have used the light and shade as in the studies of the partridge and raven to bring out the main solid forms.

The Buzzard, scarce in the greater part of England is fairly common in Wales and the west country. It is easily recognisable on the wing by its habit of soaring for hours often wheeling in circles, rising effortlessly on the ascending air-currents.

The Golden Eagle, our largest bird of prey, is practically confined to the highlands of Scotland.

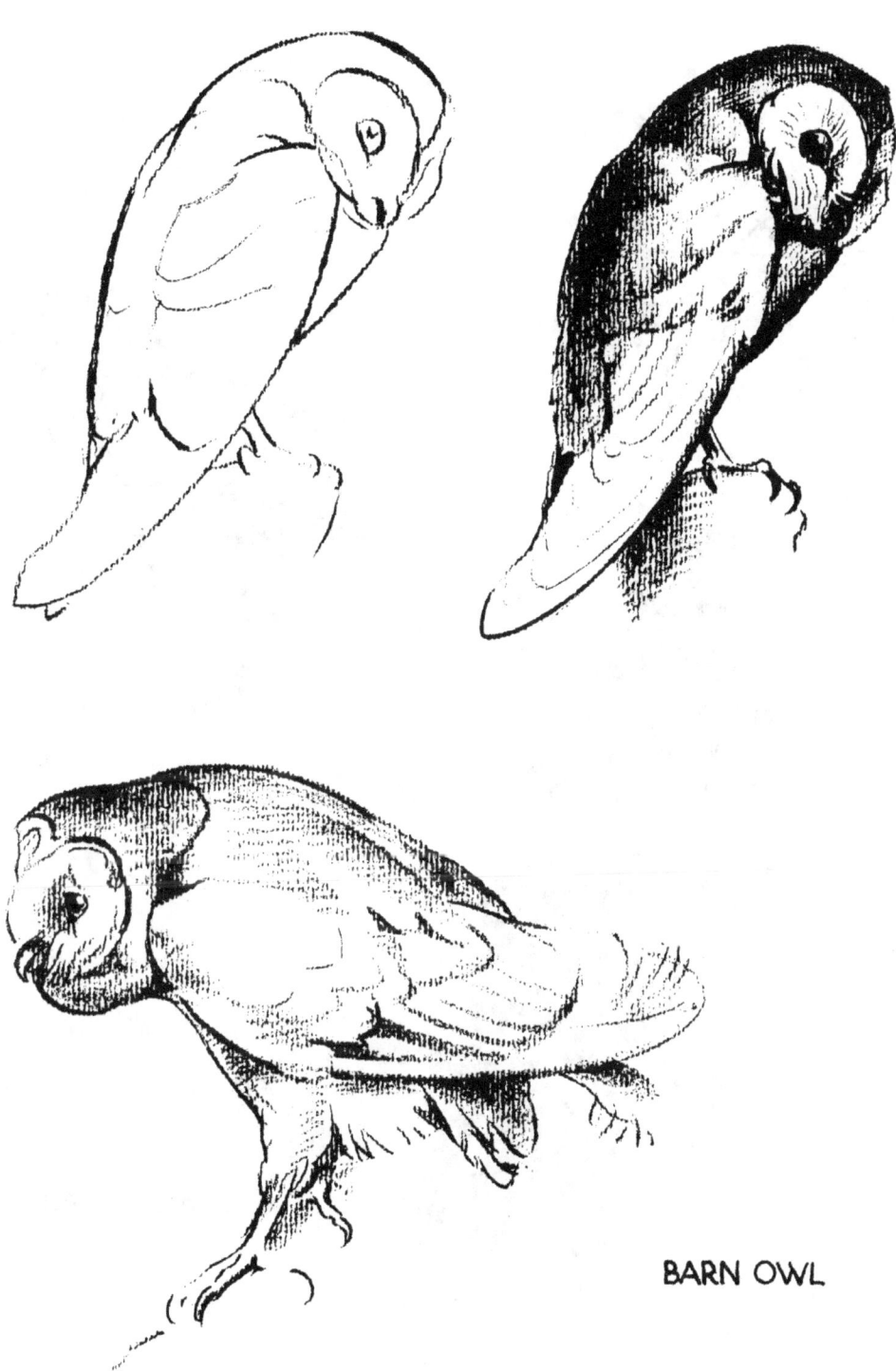

BARN OWL

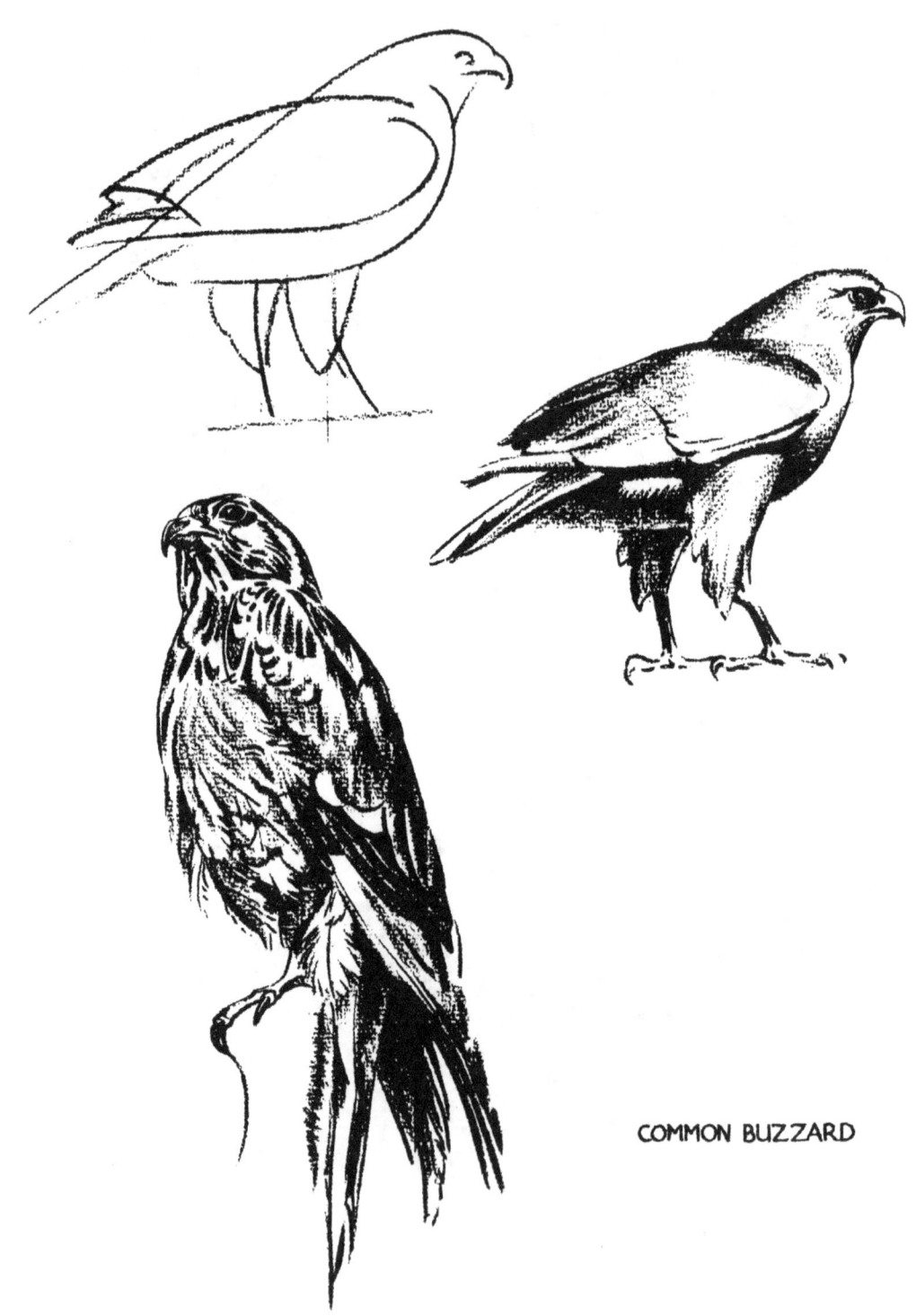

COMMON BUZZARD

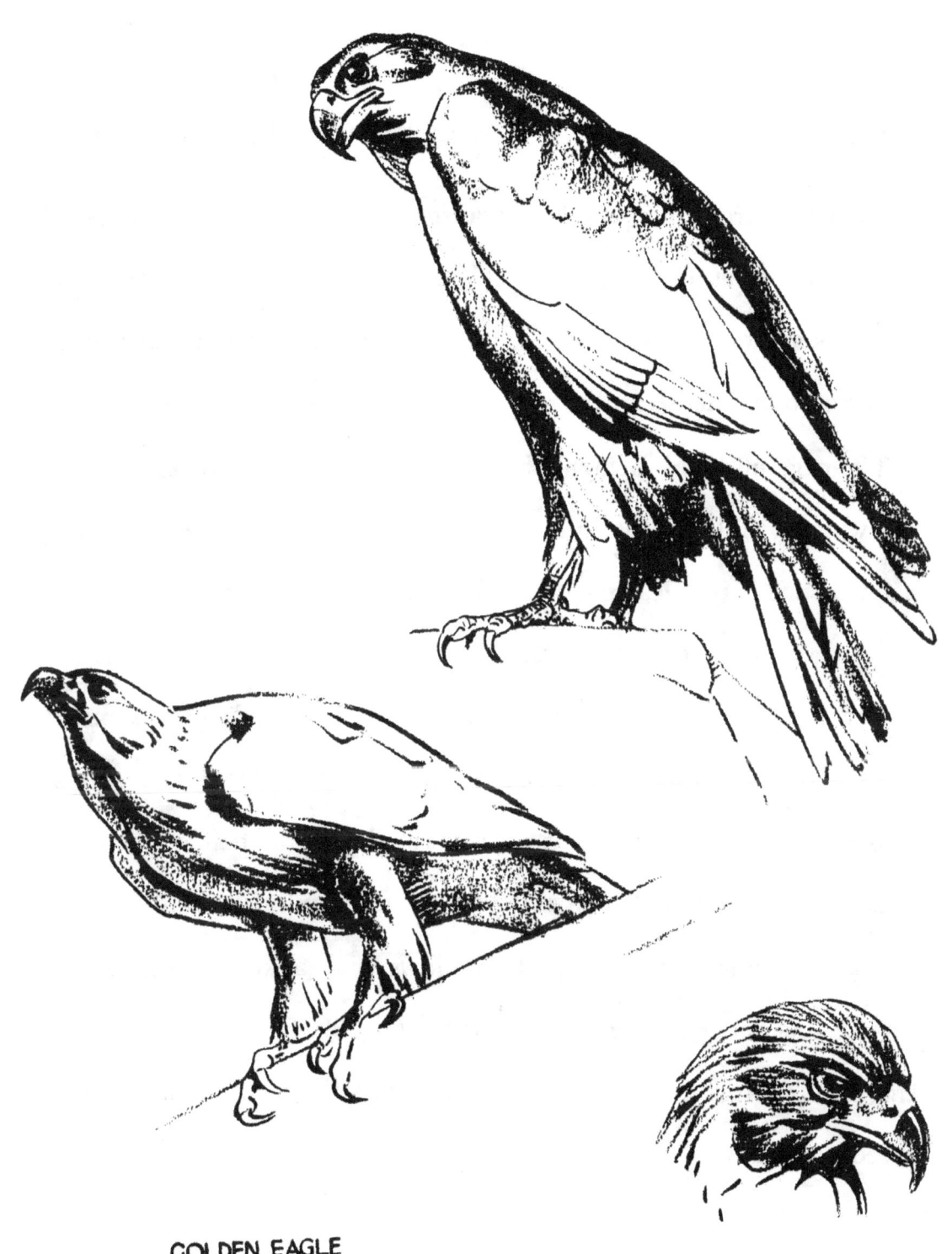

GOLDEN EAGLE

ON THE WING
GULLS — DUCK — SWALLOW AND KESTREL

Drawing birds on the wing requires endless study and hours of patient observation. At first try and get down on paper only the few lines sufficient to indicate the main position of wings in relation to body and tail, details can be added from memory afterwards.

The page of ducks in flight shows some of the positions assumed by the wings visible to the human eye. The one in the bottom-right hand corner is just leaving the water. For the first few strokes, the wings make their greatest stretch upwards, forwards and downwards— indeed sometimes the wing-tips meet above their heads in this initial stretch up—the downward pressure separates the pointed pinion tips, whose flexible ends bend almost at right angles to the shaft. The duck rises in a spiral gradually drawing up its feet under its tail.

The remaining plates are of swallows and a kestrel — note the zig-zag line about the cut of the wings and tail of the swallows. An emphasis on this characteristic always conveys a great impression of speed and dash.

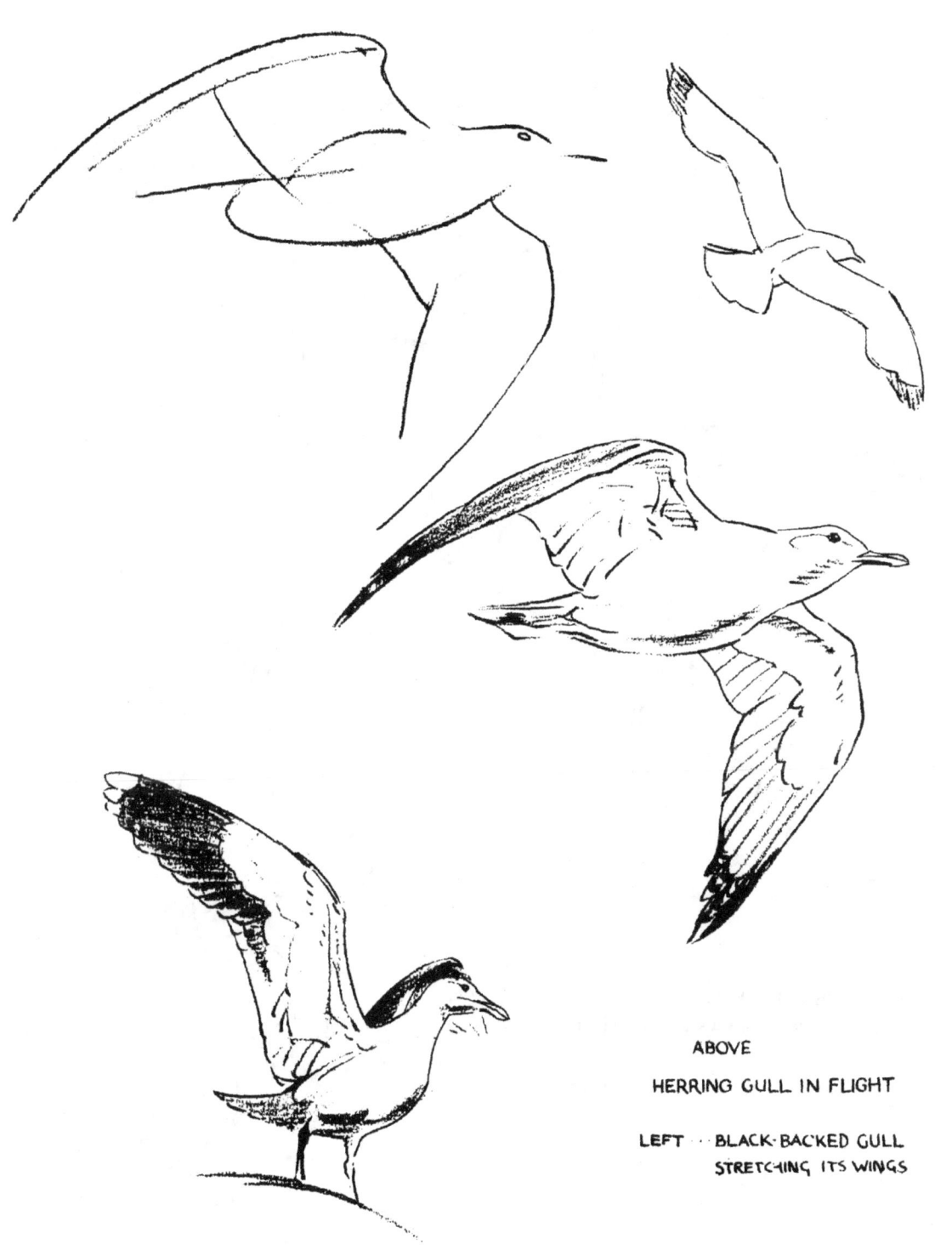

ABOVE

HERRING GULL IN FLIGHT

LEFT · · · BLACK-BACKED GULL
        STRETCHING ITS WINGS

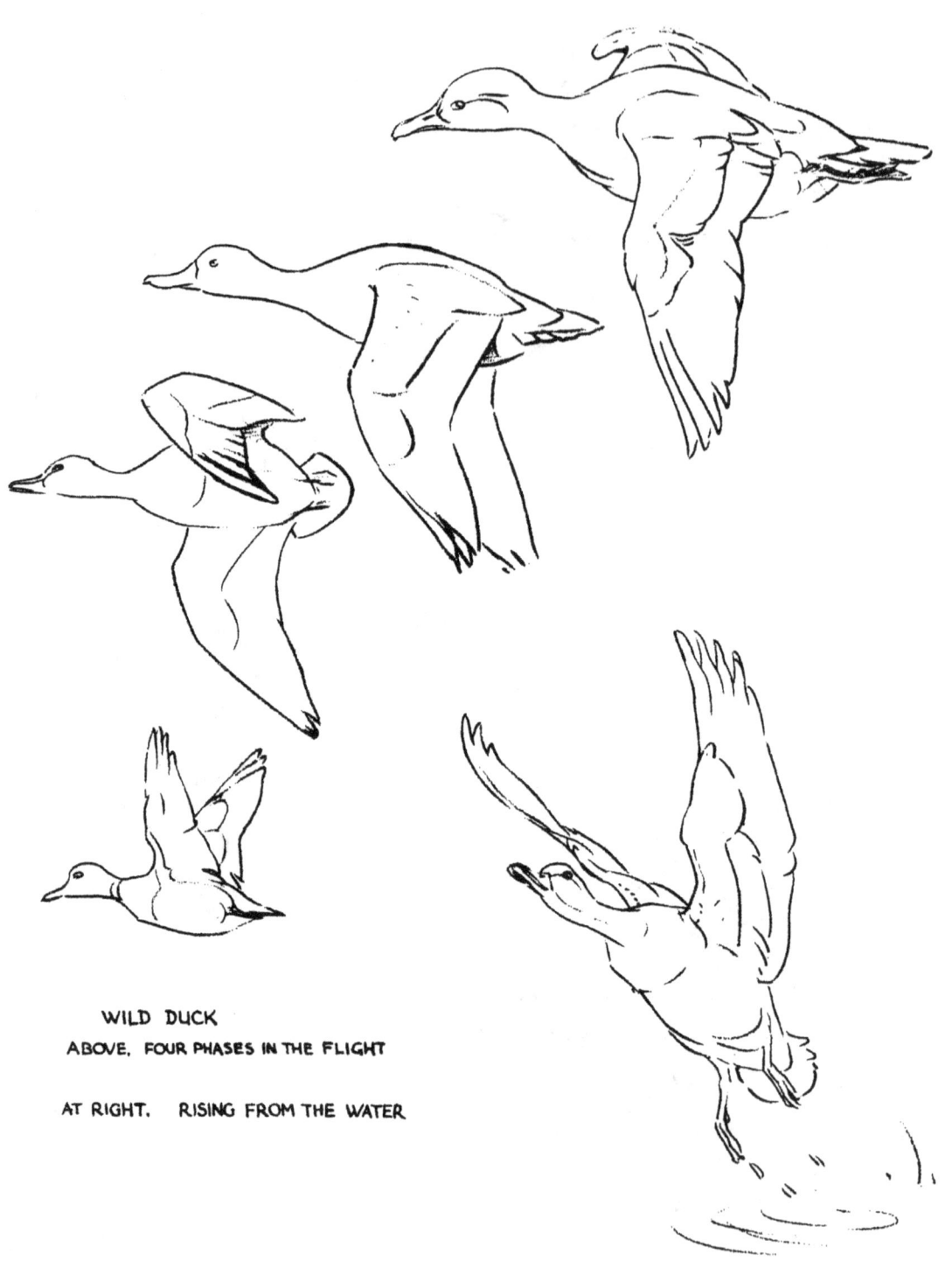

WILD DUCK

ABOVE, FOUR PHASES IN THE FLIGHT

AT RIGHT. RISING FROM THE WATER

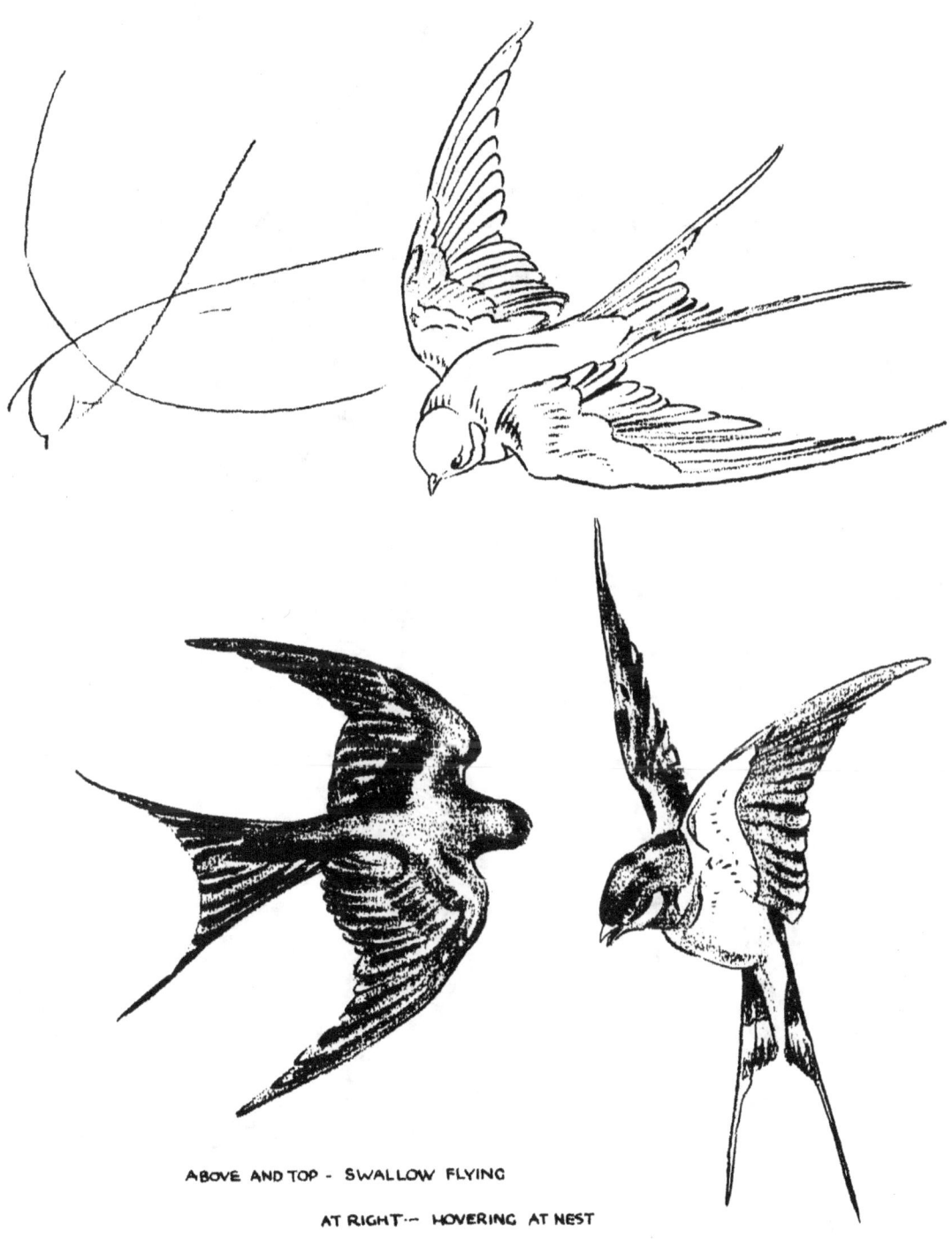

ABOVE AND TOP - SWALLOW FLYING

AT RIGHT - HOVERING AT NEST

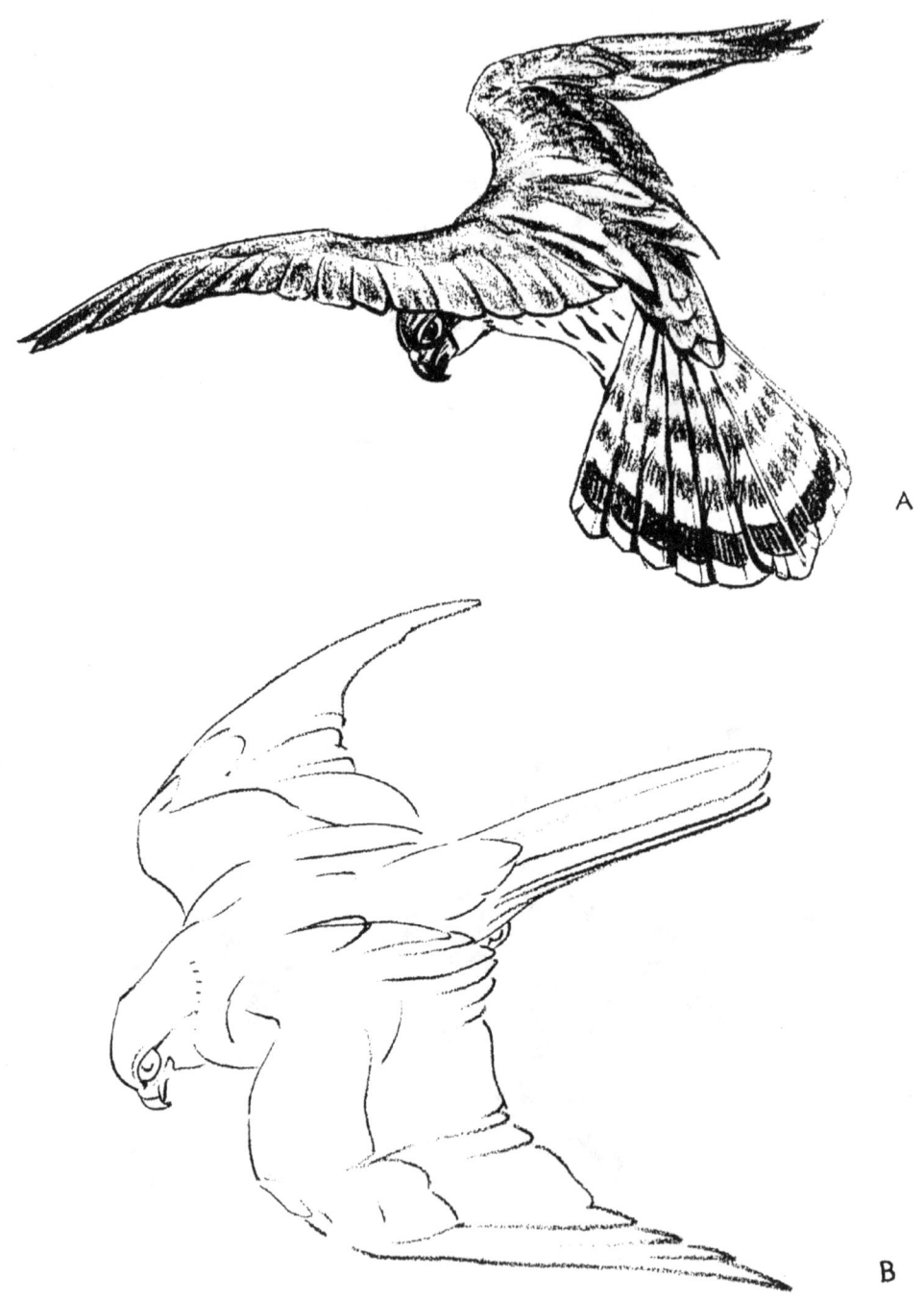

KESTREL   A   HOVERING

B   FLYING, LOOKING DOWN ON THE GROUND

MORE BIRDS
TO DRAW

by Raymond Sheppard

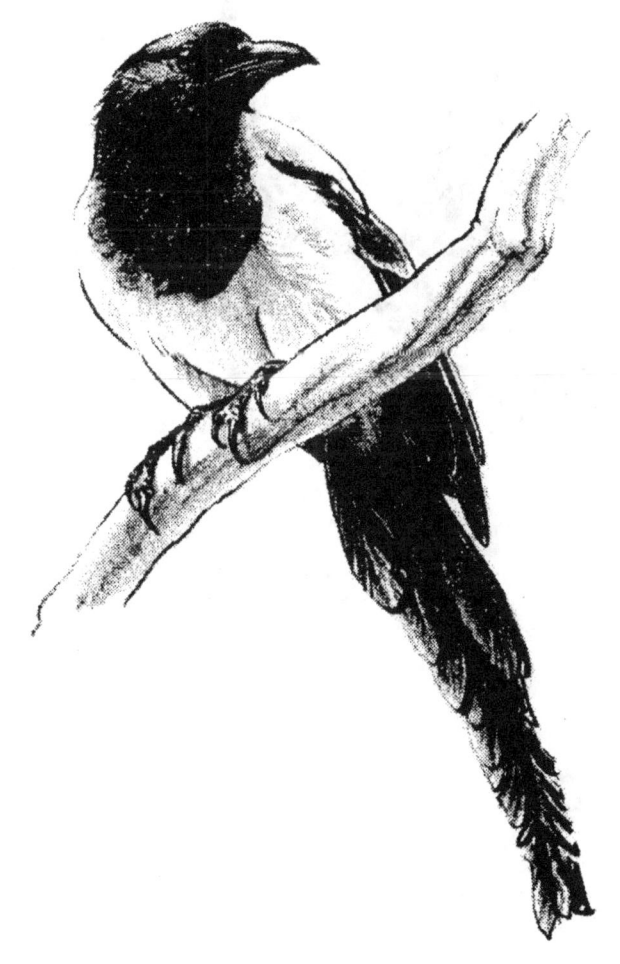

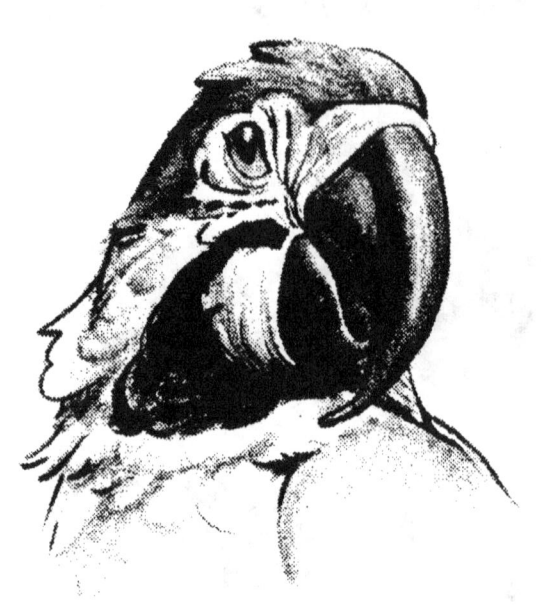

CONTENTS

INTRODUCTION	6	GREAT BIRD OF PARADISE	38
LAUGHING JACKASS	7	AUSTRALIAN LYRE BIRD	39
SIMPLE SHAPES AND		HOW BIRDS FLY	42
STRUCTURE	11	DRAWING AT A ROOKERY	48
MAKING A START	14	MAGPIES	50
FINCHS	15	JAYS	51
BLUE TITS AND GREAT TITS	16	KESTRELS AND CONDORS	52
QUEEN ALEXANDRA'S PARRAKEETS	17	OWLS	54
FLIGHTLESS BIRDS	18	BACKGROUND STUDIES	56
CASSOWARY	20	JAVA SPARROWS	58
THE DODO	21	BLACKBIRD	59
PENGUINS	22	NIGHTINGALE	60
DRAWING WITH A BRUSH	24	GREAT SPOTTED WOODPECKER	61
PHEASANTS	26	PICTURES FROM YOUR STUDIES	62
KALIJ PHEASANT	27		
TURKEY	28		
GUINEA FOWL	29		
SOME NESTS	30		
BABY BIRDS	32		
THE STUDY OF DETAIL	34		
DOVES AND PIGEONS	36		

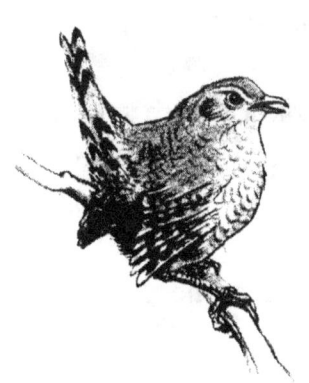

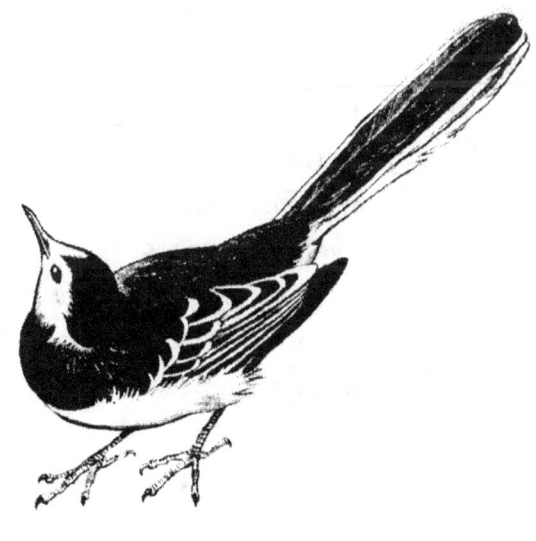

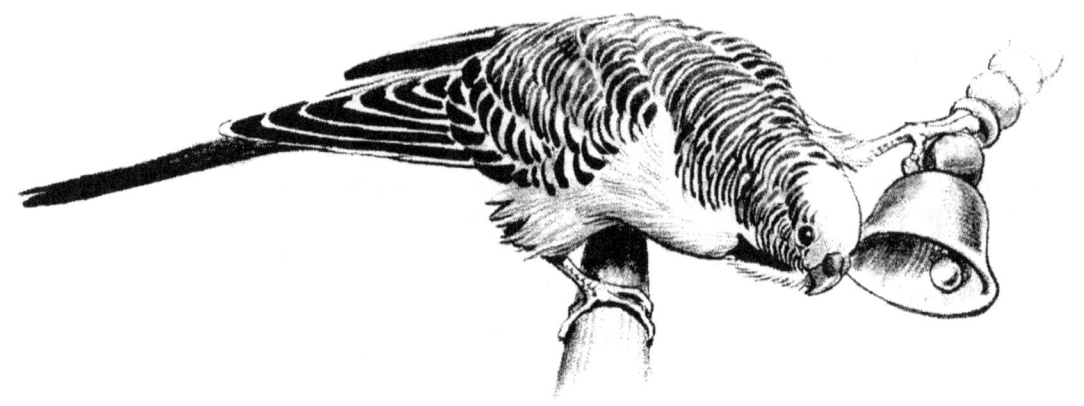

INTRODUCTION

THOUSANDS of birds of different species throng the air, the land and the water—therefore in choosing a few studies to amplify my previous book *How to draw Birds* I have limited myself to birds other than water birds, as I think they would need a volume all to themselves. Penguins, which find a place here, are the exception. They are birds that I have enjoyed drawing and studying either in a zoo, a garden or in their natural wild state. The choice is purely personal and I am sure to have omitted some of your favourites.

Artists look for form and colour in nature. We cannot deal with colour here, but only suggest it by texture and tone, so I have shown birds whose form, rather than colour, appeals to me, or whose pattern is decorative or exciting.

The shape and size of a bird can vary enormously. Sometimes looking

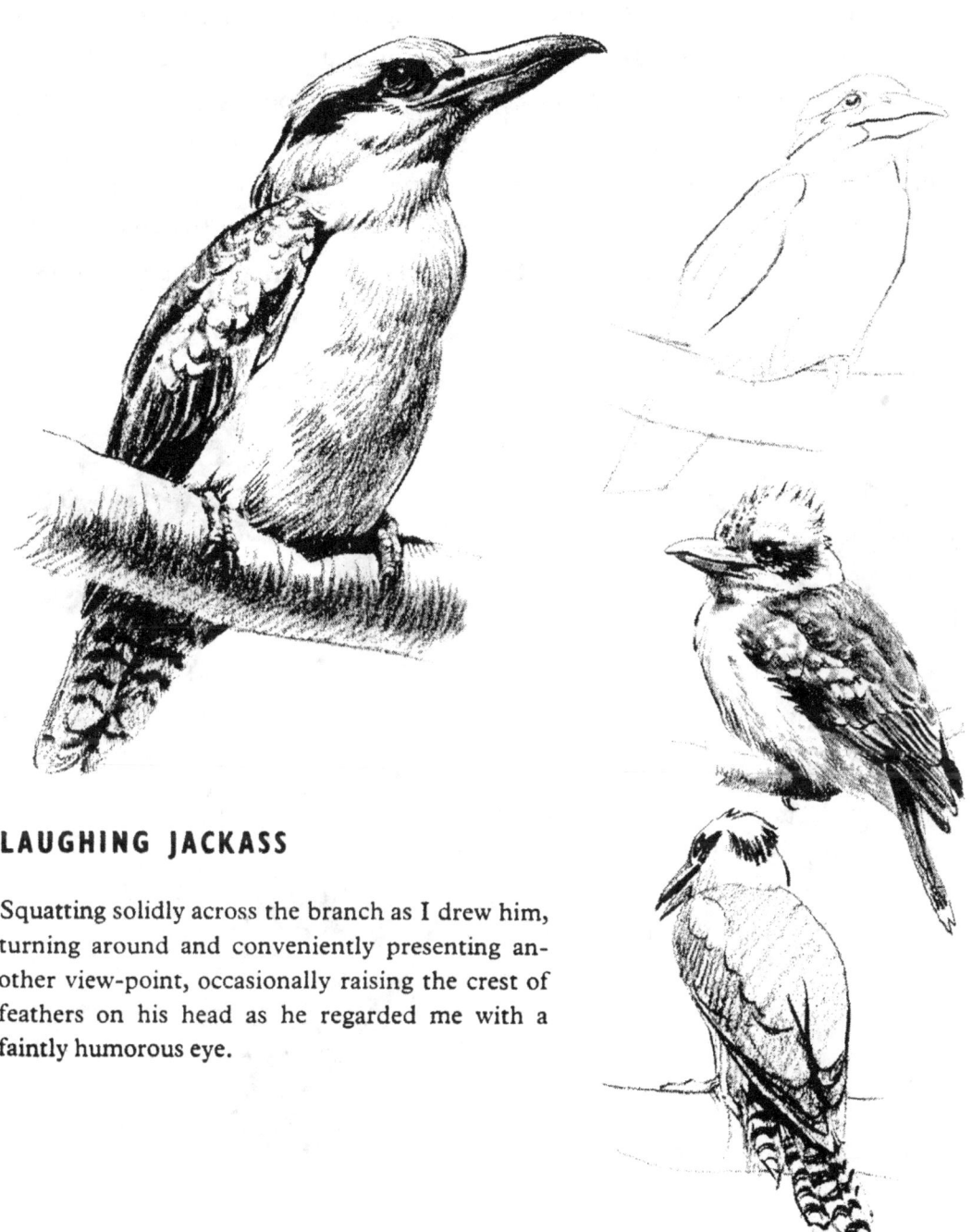

LAUGHING JACKASS

Squatting solidly across the branch as I drew him, turning around and conveniently presenting another view-point, occasionally raising the crest of feathers on his head as he regarded me with a faintly humorous eye.

sleek and slender, the same bird, by fluffing out its feathers can become quite round. The small wing span of a humming bird is scarcely as wide as the eye of an ostrich. This variety of size and shape is seen in every detail. Beaks are as varied in shape as are the tools we use—some are pincers to crack nuts: some are hooks to tear meat: others look like a pick-axe.

Feet, likewise, vary in size and function from the great two-toed hoof-like foot of the ostrich, a bird that can run faster than a horse, to the tiny

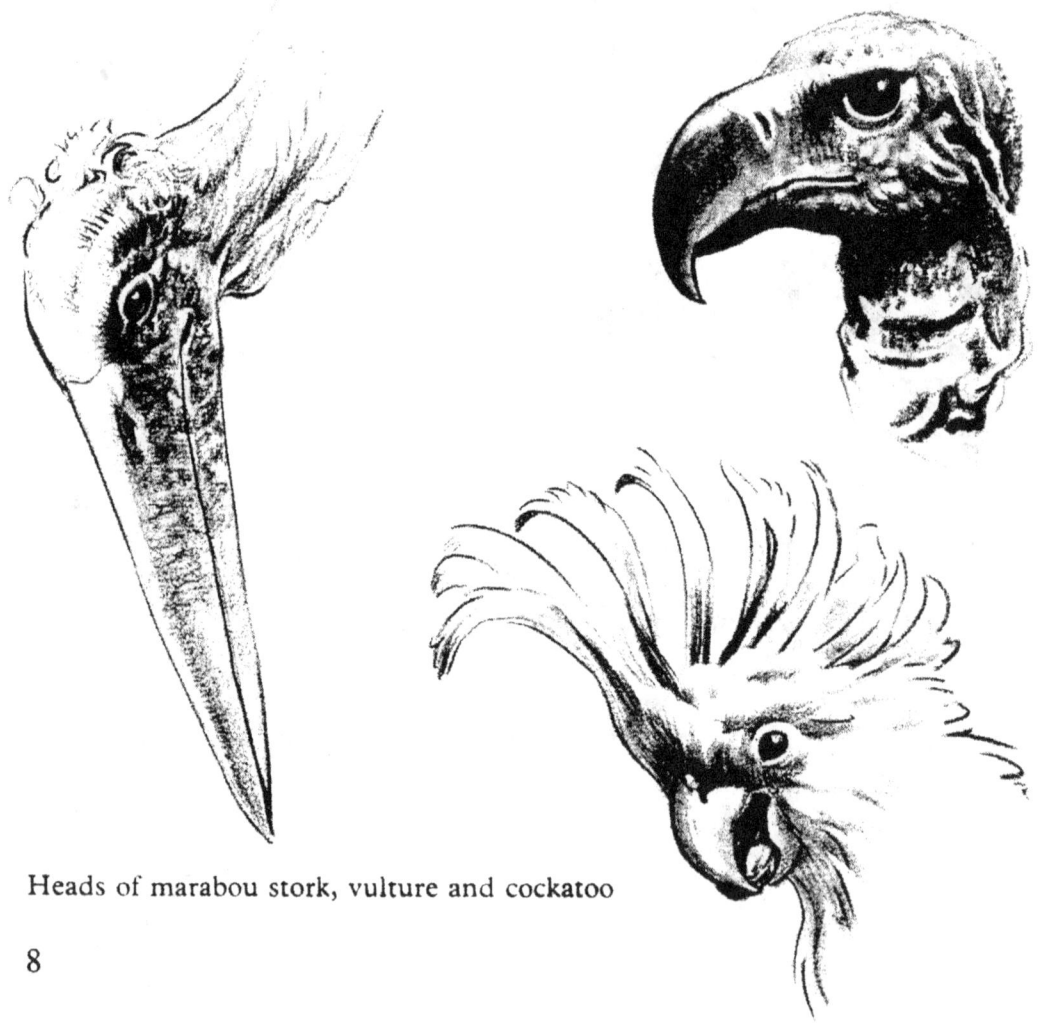

Heads of marabou stork, vulture and cockatoo

8

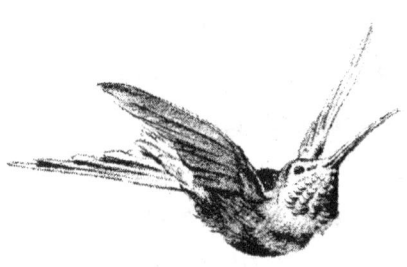

Humming bird

claws of the swift which spends most
of its time on the wing, and clings
only to cliffs, houses or twigs high
above the ground. I have been able
to show only a tiny cross-section of
this infinite variety.

Ostrich

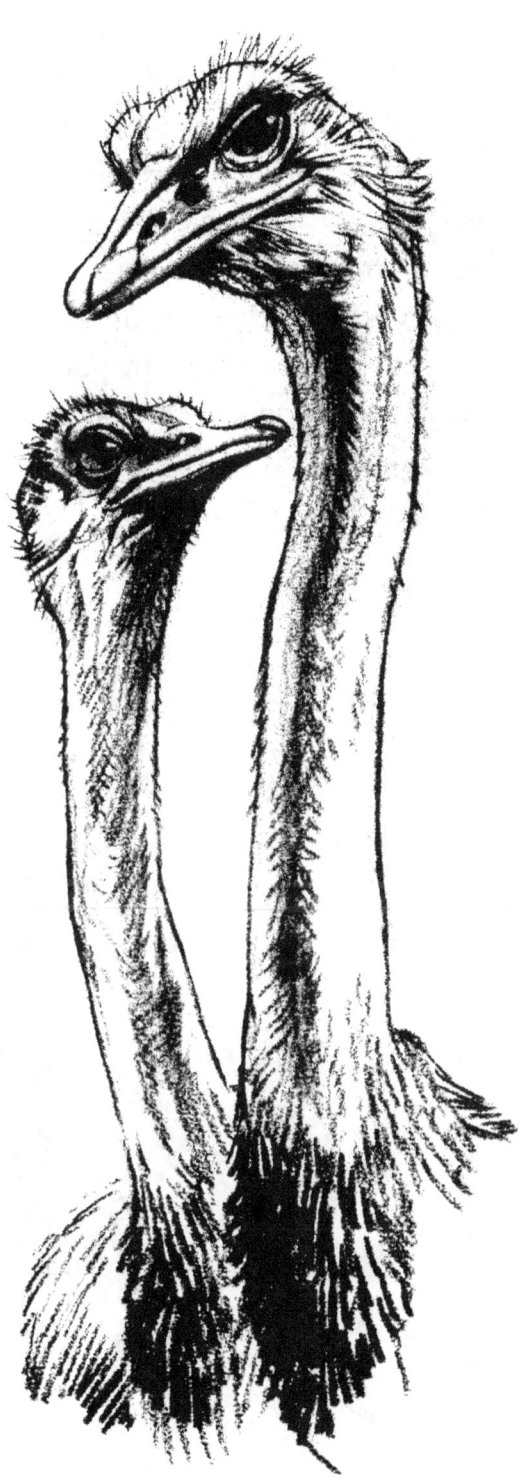

As this is a book about drawing I have shown you drawings in a variety of stages, some slight, some incomplete even, and some swift and summary. They do not all pretend to be highly finished and accurate natural history records. I have drawn that particular aspect of a bird which appeals to me; sometimes shape, sometimes pattern and texture and sometimes a briefly held attitude. They are done in a variety of media, in carbon pencil or conté, or in pen, pen and wash or in wash alone. They constitute the bulk of this book, because I believe that drawings can say more than words and I hope they will stimulate you to discover for yourself the joys of drawing these lovely creatures.

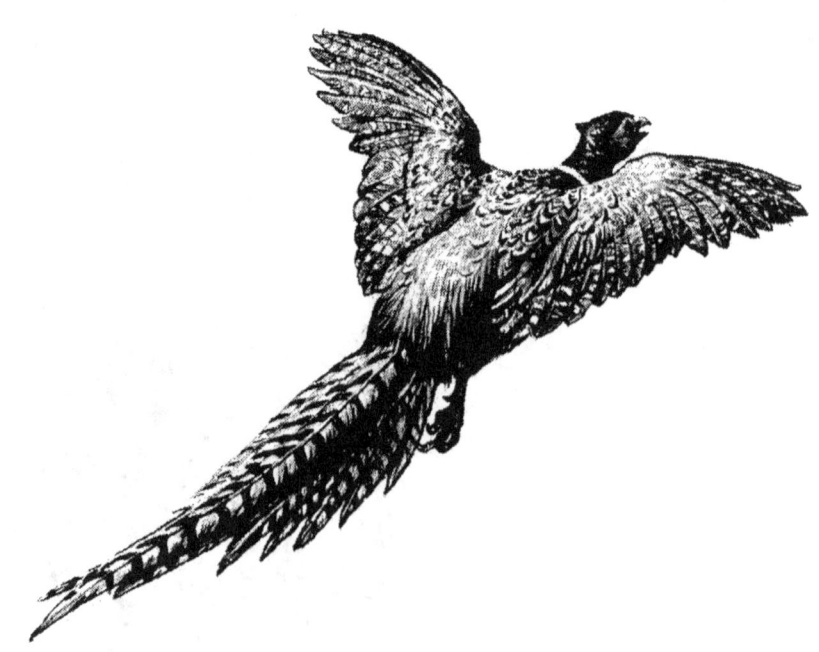

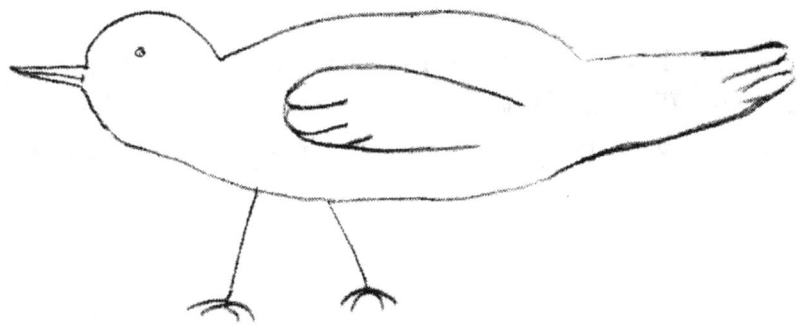

SIMPLE SHAPES & STRUCTURE

HERE is a drawing by a child of eight. It is a simple memory drawing in outline showing all the important parts of a bird—no superfluous detail and really very good. Now we can learn a lot from this drawing because, by using shapes just as simple as a child's, but with more knowledge of structure, we can produce a fair representation of a bird.

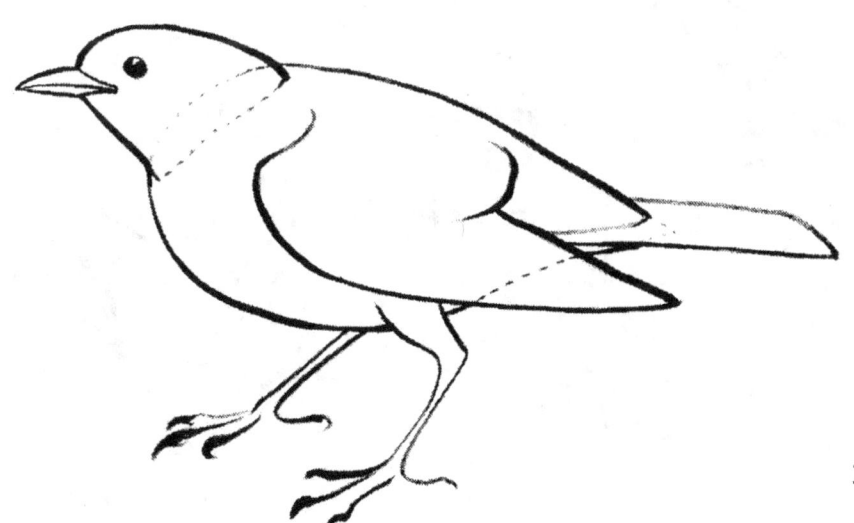

Here I have shown the various parts of a bird reduced to simple, solid shapes. When it is understood just how simply the bird's form is built, it can be visualised in any position and drawn from any point of view.

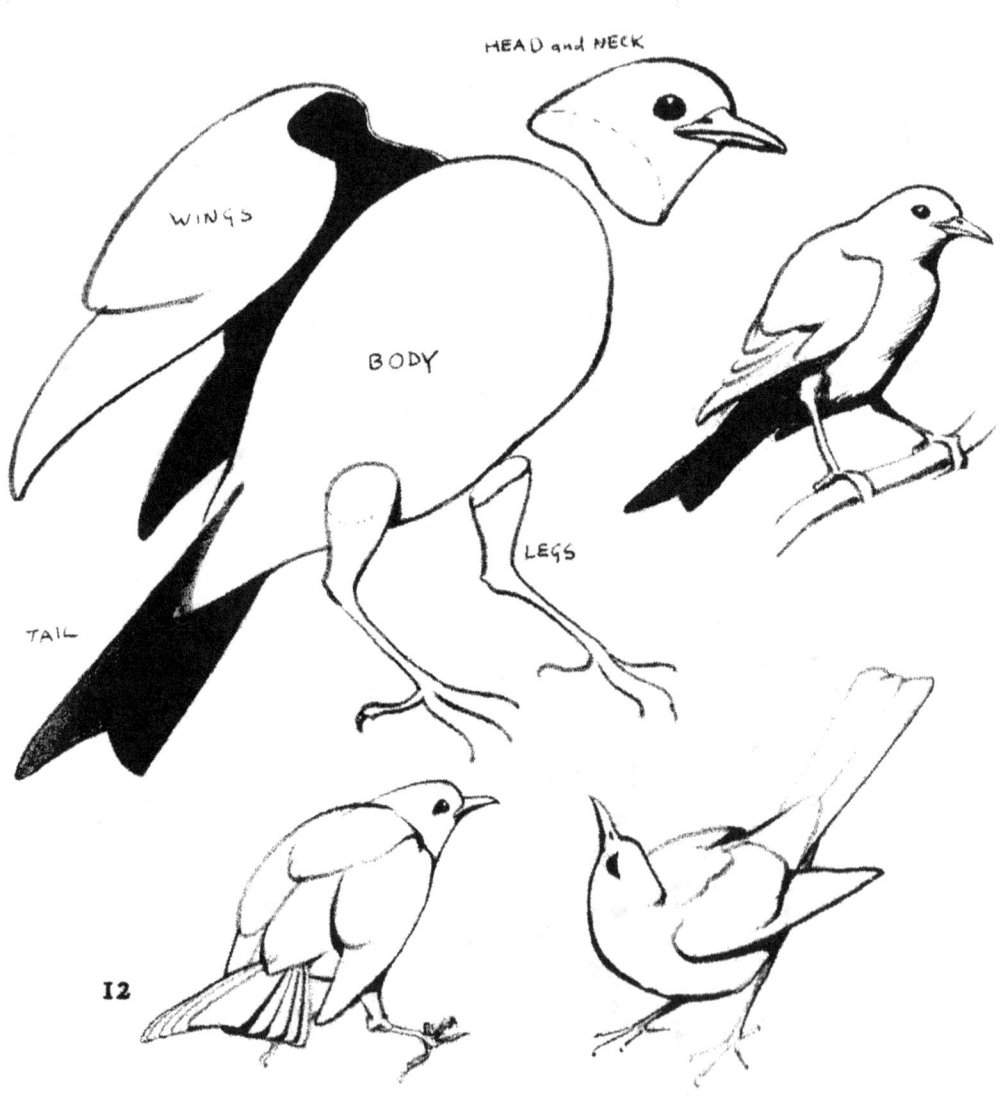

HEAD and NECK

WINGS

BODY

LEGS

TAIL

12

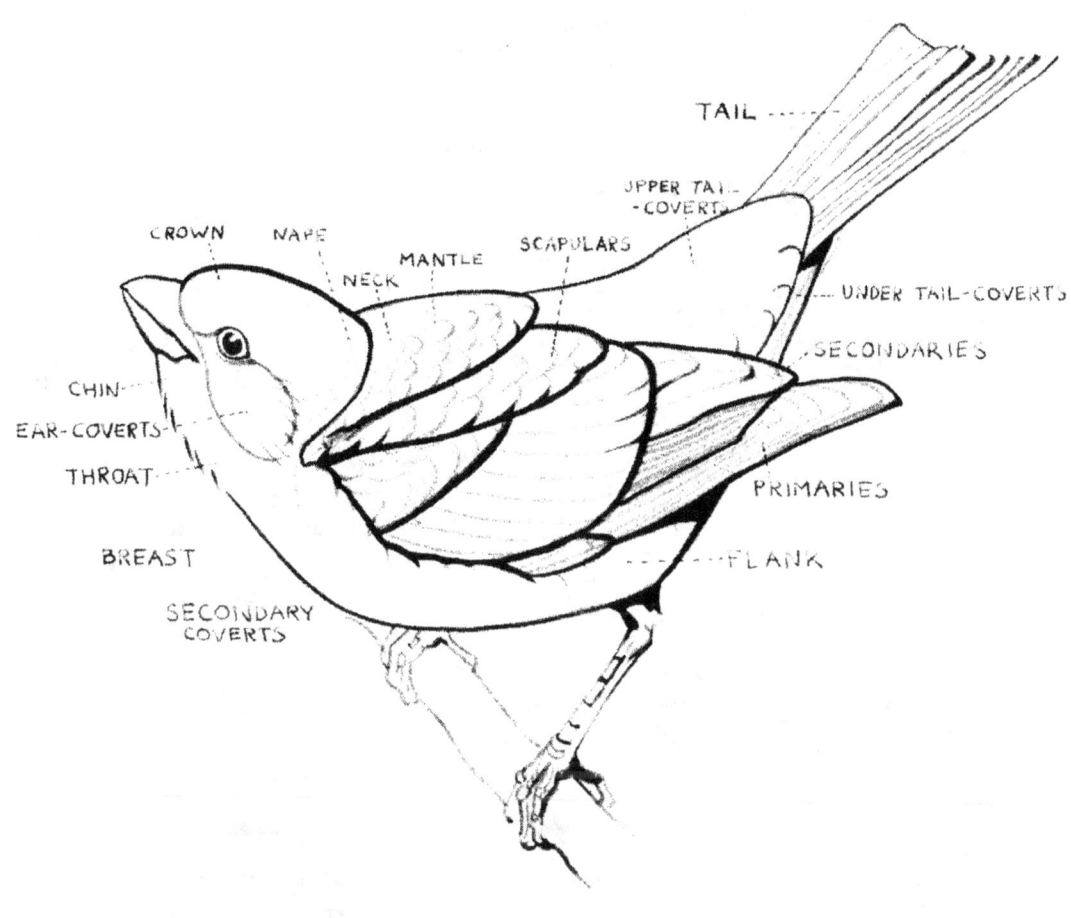

TAIL

UPPER TAIL
-COVERTS

CROWN   NAPE
                    MANTLE   SCAPULARS
             NECK

UNDER TAIL-COVERTS

SECONDARIES

CHIN
EAR-COVERTS
THROAT

PRIMARIES

BREAST

FLANK

SECONDARY
COVERTS

A little more now.

This diagram shows these parts in a little more detail as they are in nature. The feathers are in clearly-seen groups which I have named for you. Now we are ready to draw from living birds. On the next page I have shown you a diagram and some studies from life.

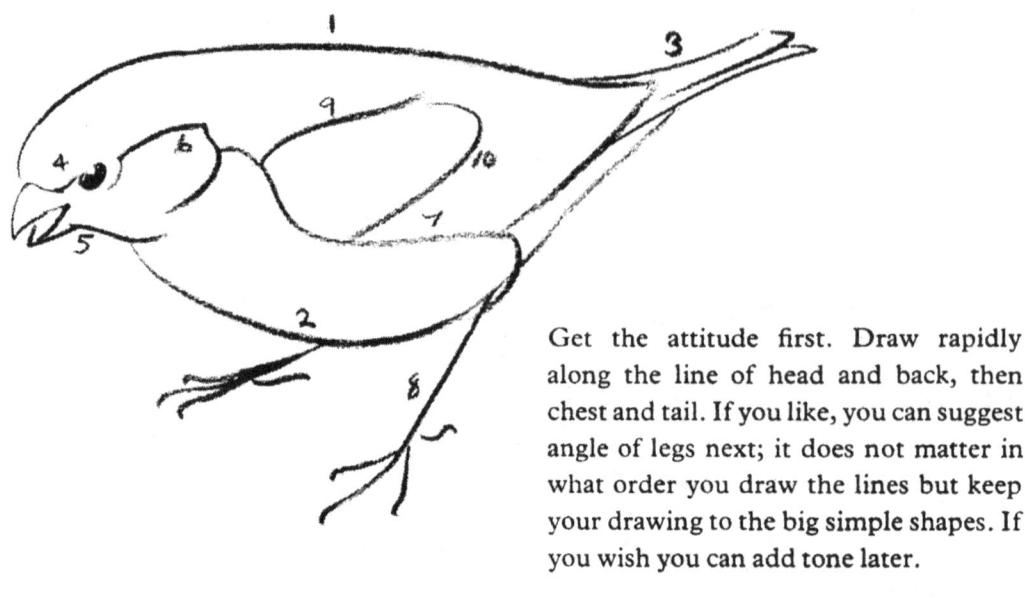

Get the attitude first. Draw rapidly along the line of head and back, then chest and tail. If you like, you can suggest angle of legs next; it does not matter in what order you draw the lines but keep your drawing to the big simple shapes. If you wish you can add tone later.

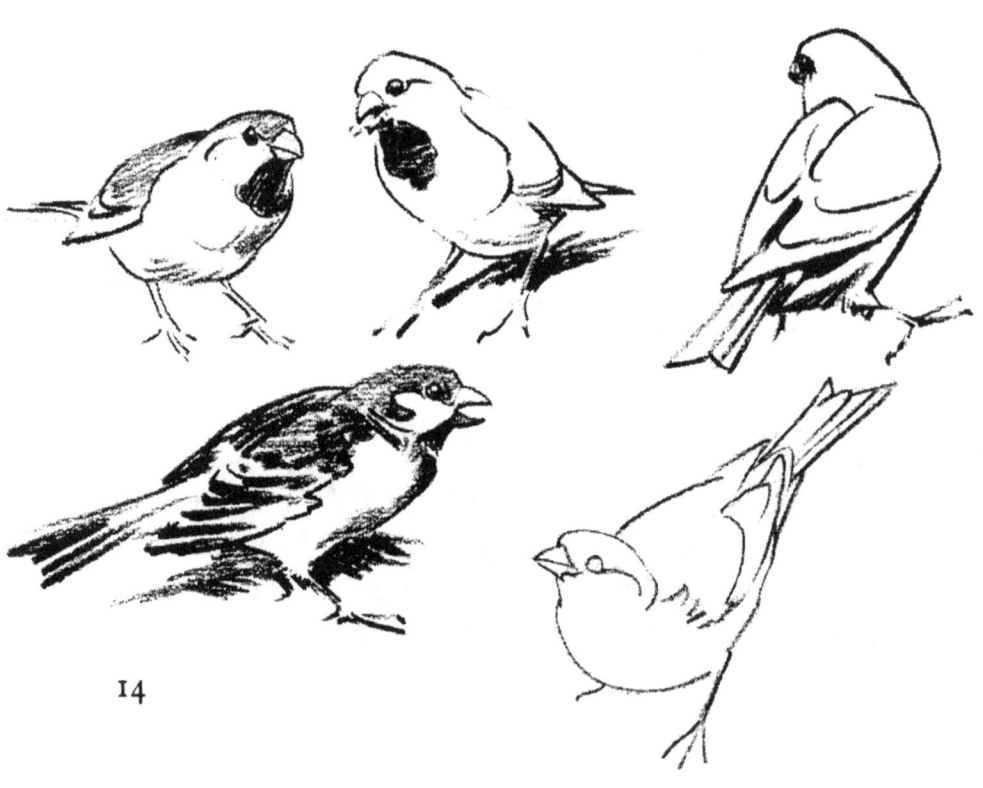

14

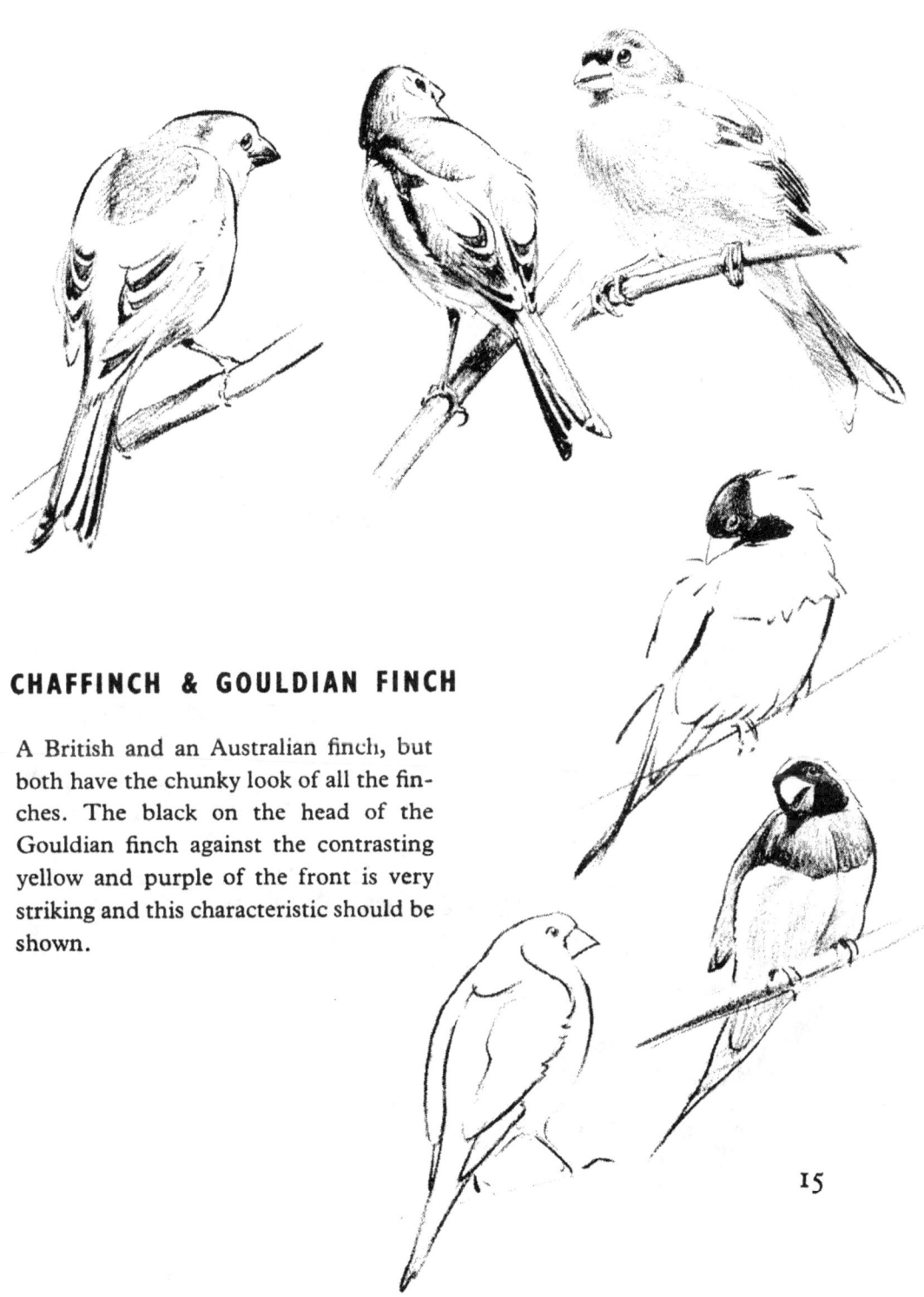

CHAFFINCH & GOULDIAN FINCH

A British and an Australian finch, but
both have the chunky look of all the finches. The black on the head of the
Gouldian finch against the contrasting
yellow and purple of the front is very
striking and this characteristic should be
shown.

15

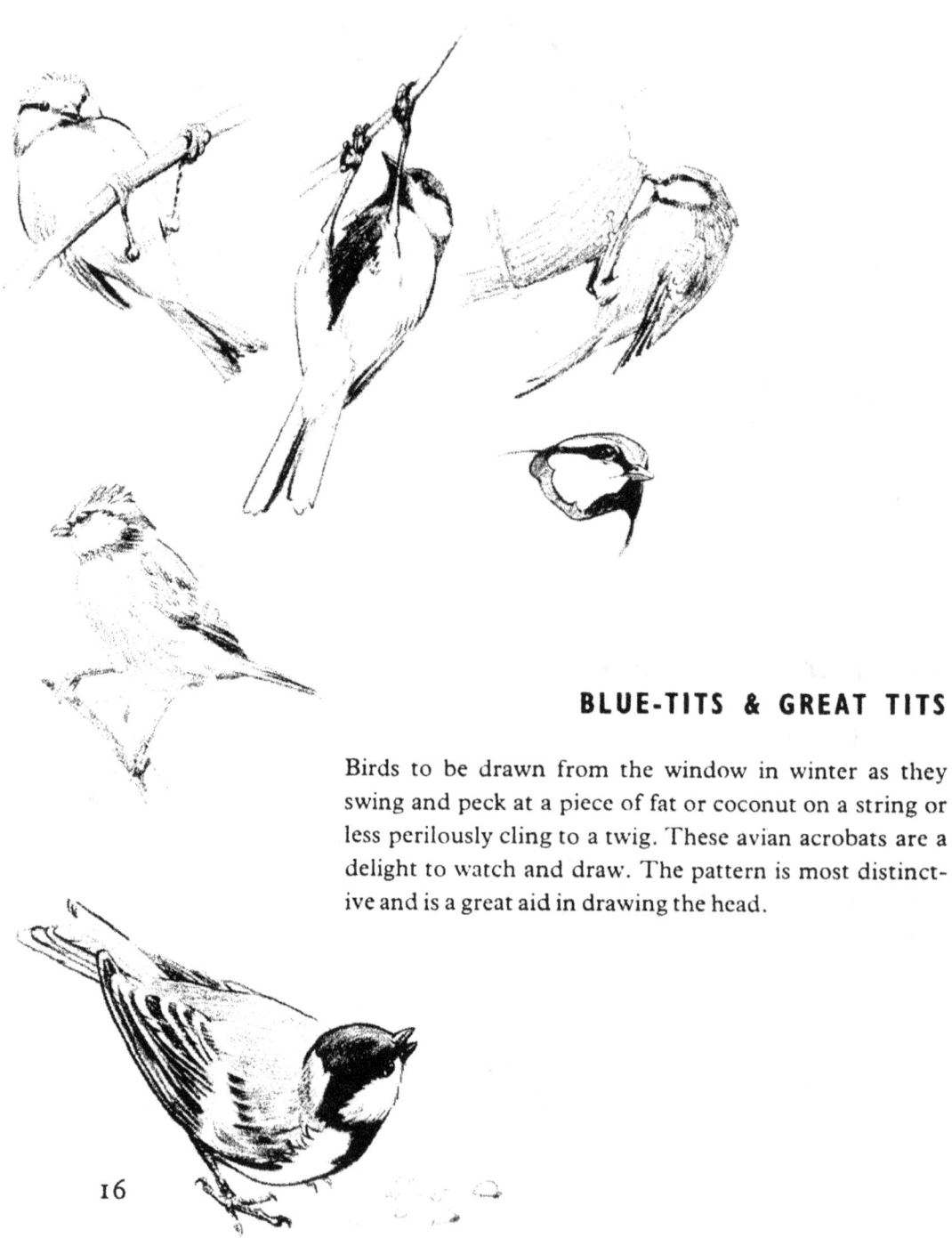

BLUE-TITS & GREAT TITS

Birds to be drawn from the window in winter as they swing and peck at a piece of fat or coconut on a string or less perilously cling to a twig. These avian acrobats are a delight to watch and draw. The pattern is most distinctive and is a great aid in drawing the head.

16

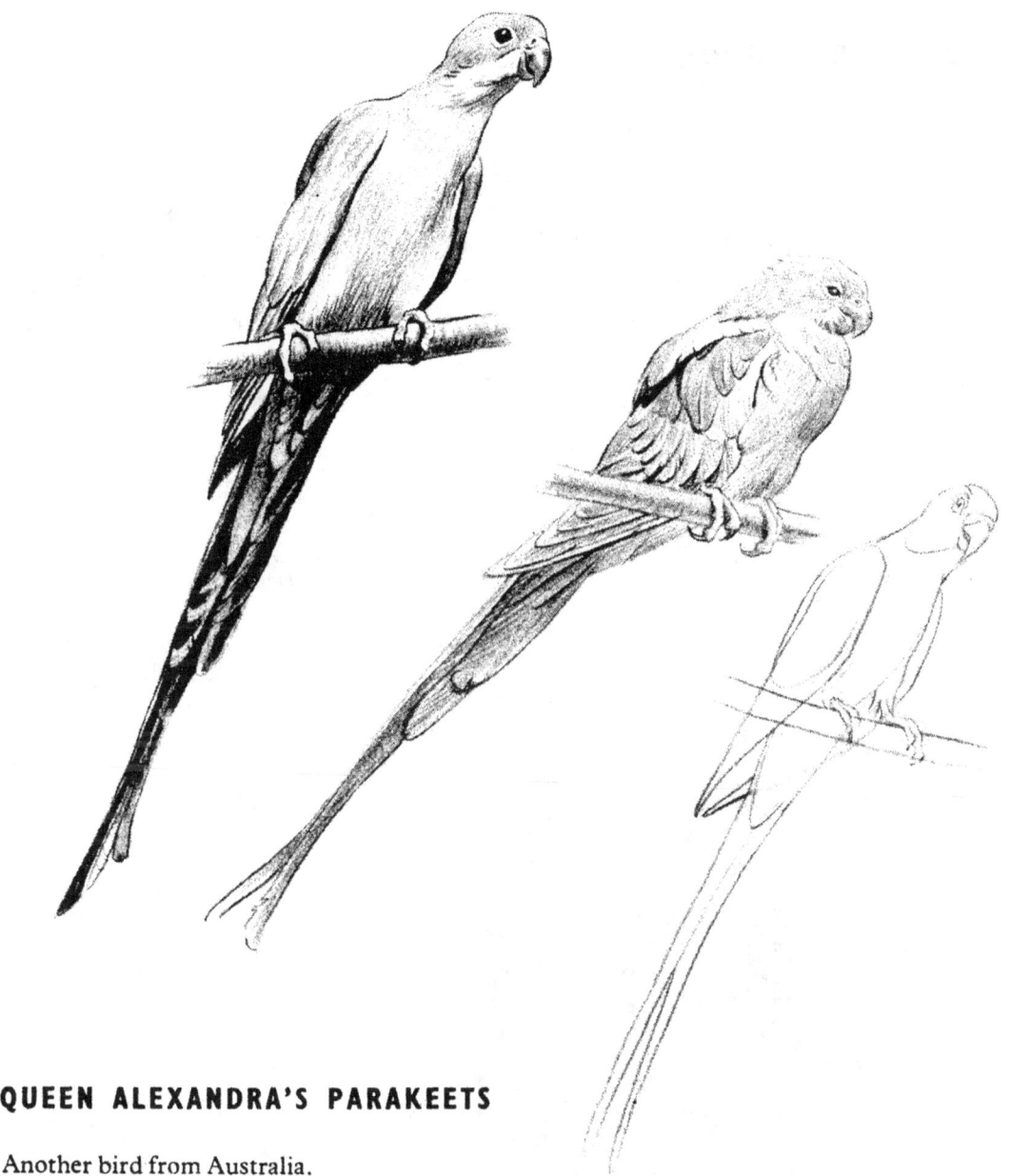

QUEEN ALEXANDRA'S PARAKEETS

Another bird from Australia.

These drawings show the same bird. In one case the feathers are loosened, the neck drawn in, giving a much fatter shape.

FLIGHTLESS BIRDS

Some birds have lost the power of flight. Their wings have become smaller and their legs larger. Indeed, in the kiwi of New Zealand the wings have almost disappeared, being completely hidden by the plumage of the back. This plumage is rather like long coarse hair. The legs and thighs are very strong and quite large. Kiwi's are unique in having the nostrils placed at the tip of the beak. Its shape can vary from a ball when it is sitting quietly, to something quite different when

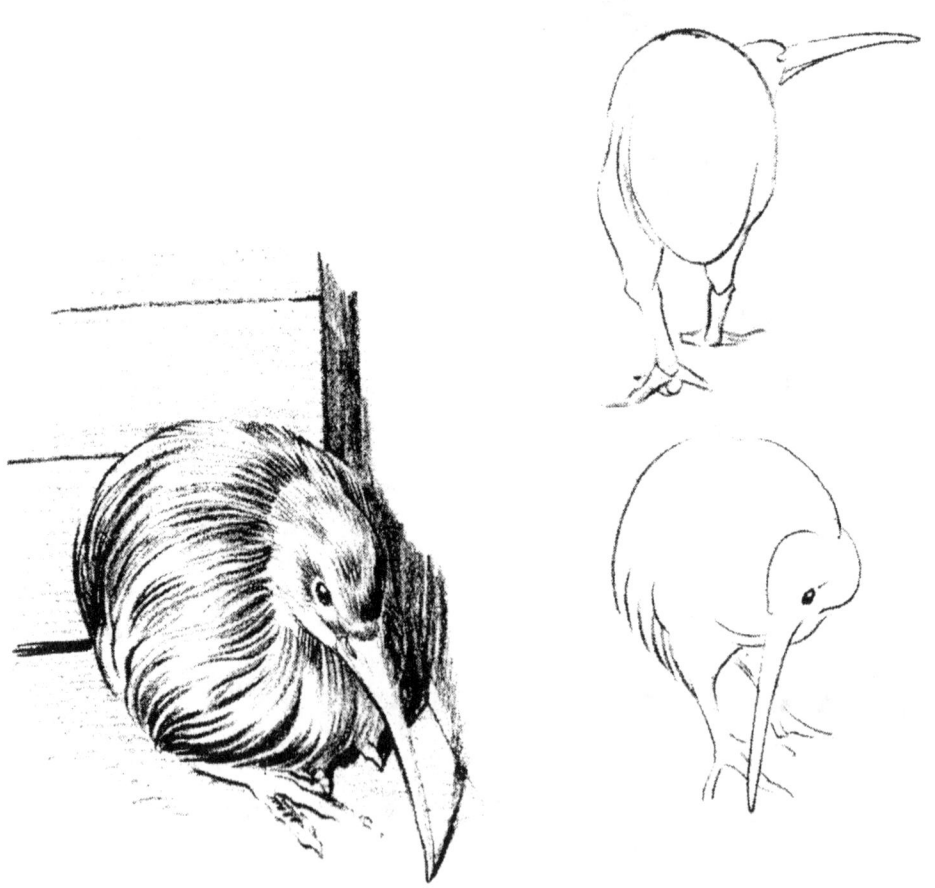

18

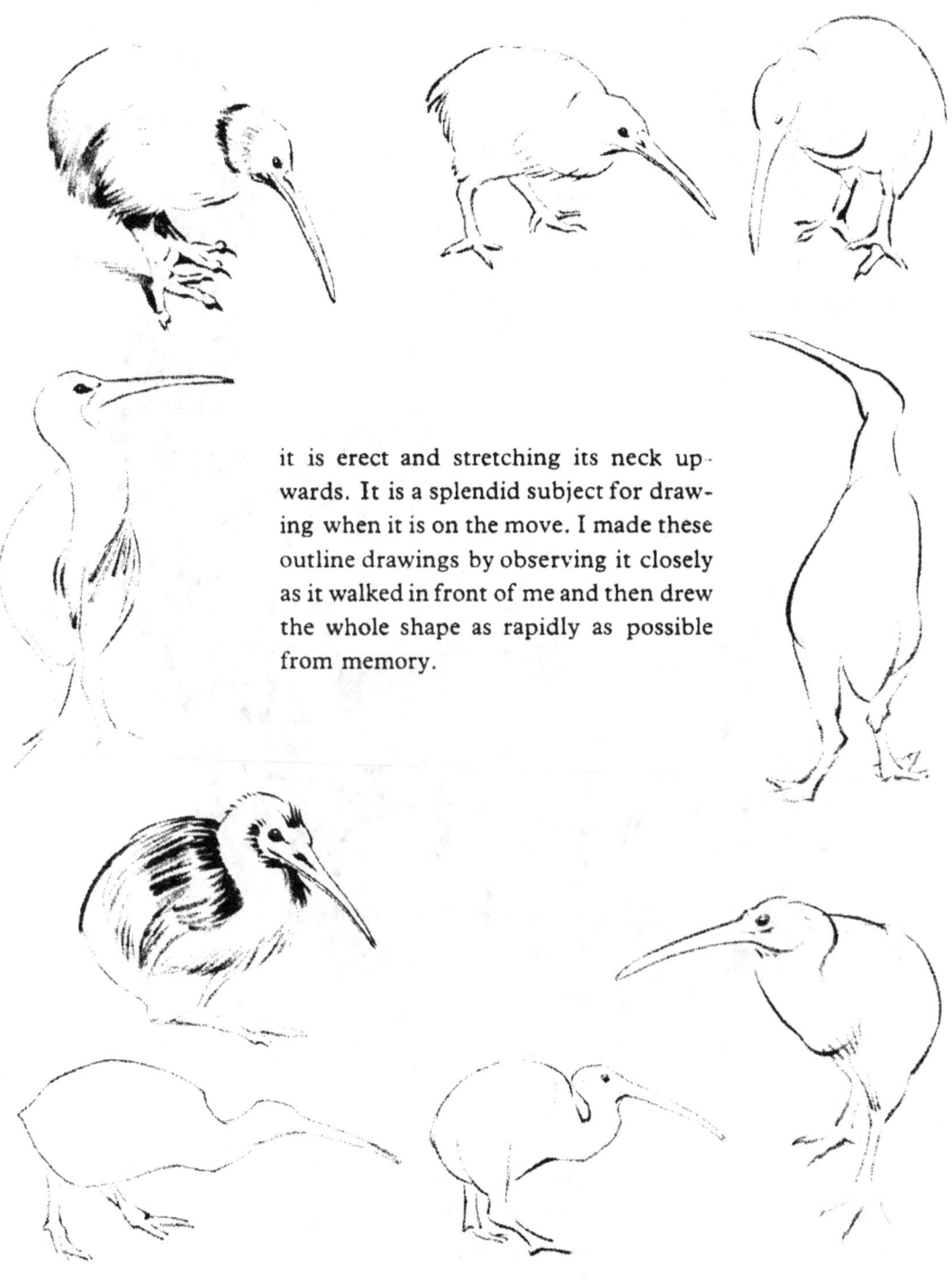

it is erect and stretching its neck up-wards. It is a splendid subject for draw-ing when it is on the move. I made these outline drawings by observing it closely as it walked in front of me and then drew the whole shape as rapidly as possible from memory.

THE CASSOWARY

A flightless bird like the kiwi with the feathers long and pointed. The brilliant scarlet and blue of the head cannot be shown here, but of particular note is the strange bony crest on the skull. This bird has three toes whereas the ostrich has only two.

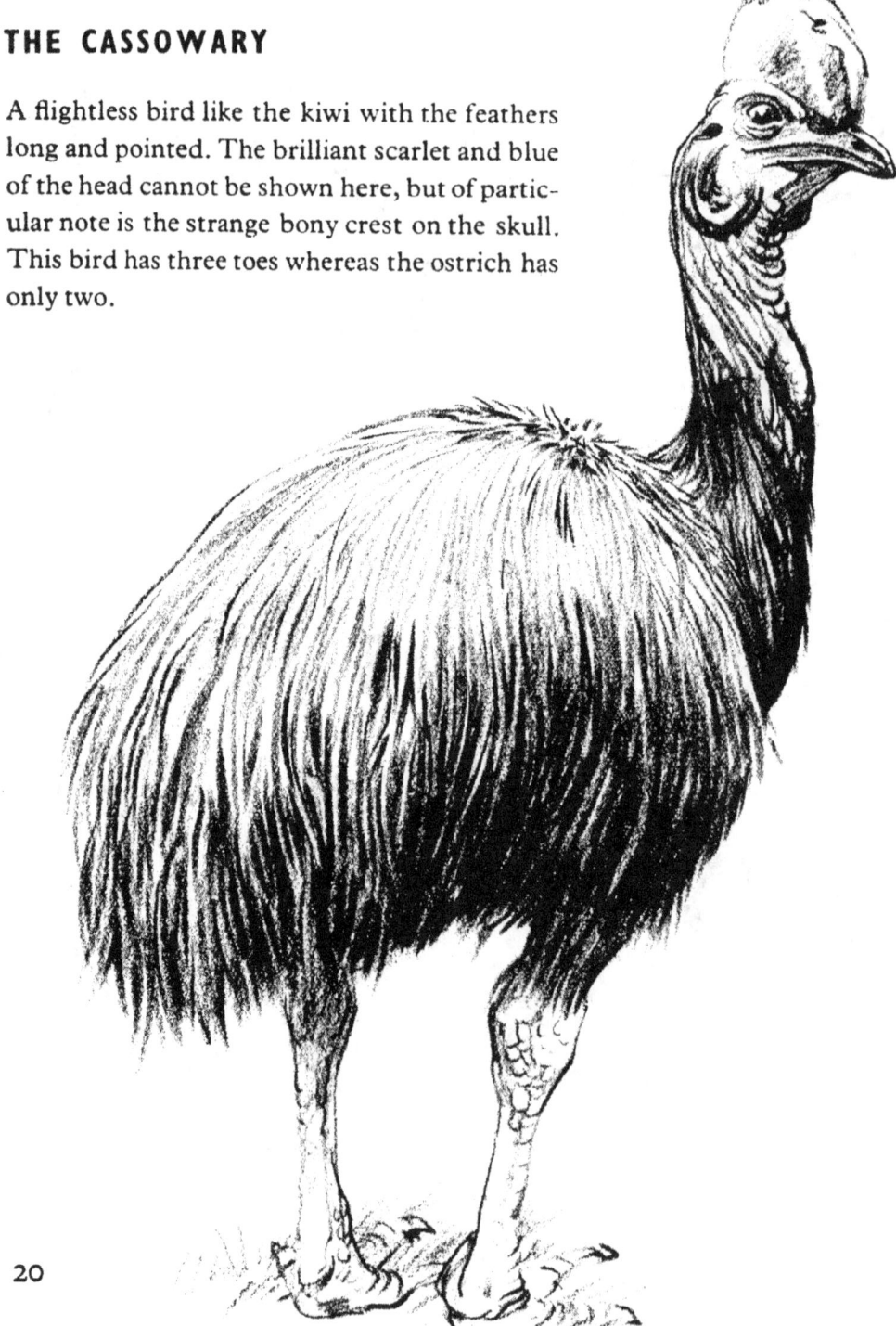

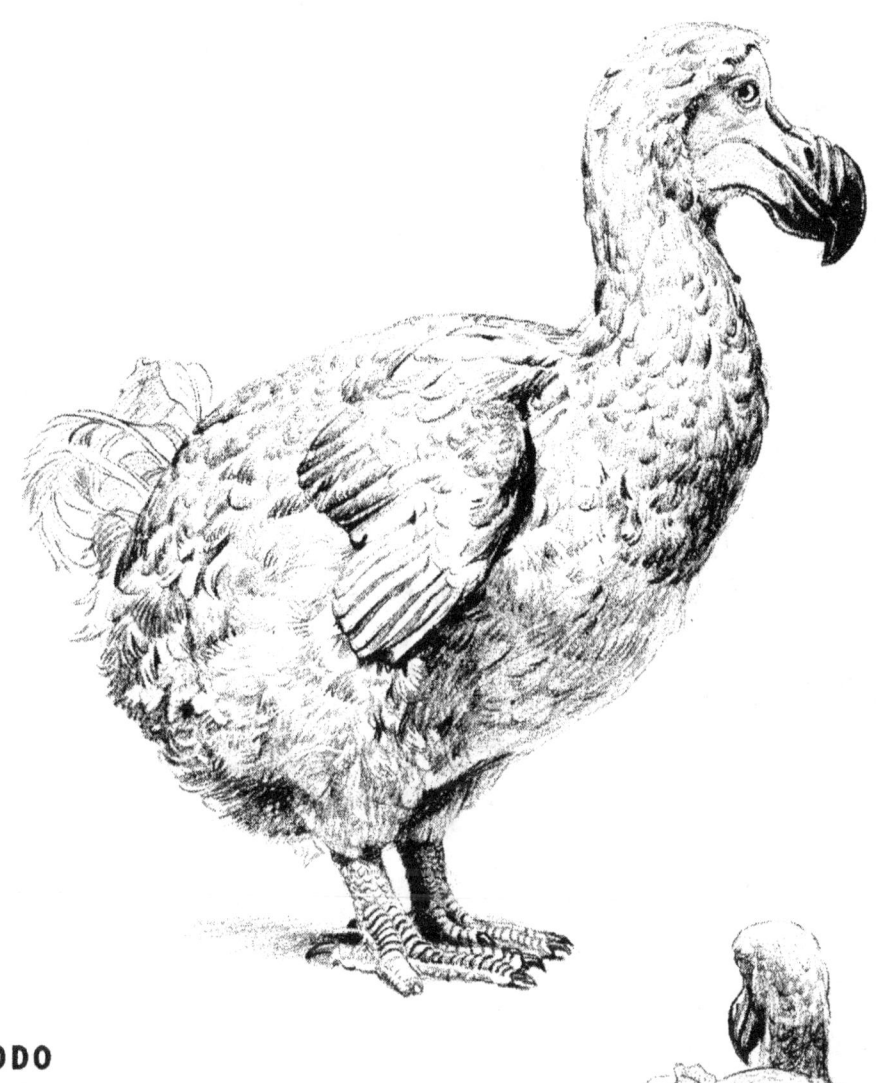

THE DODO

Well known to all who have read *Alice in Wonderland*,
the dodo is actually a near relative of the pigeon.
These large but defenceless birds that lived on the
island of Mauritius became extinct in 1691.
These drawings were made from a model
at the Natural History Museum, South Kensington.

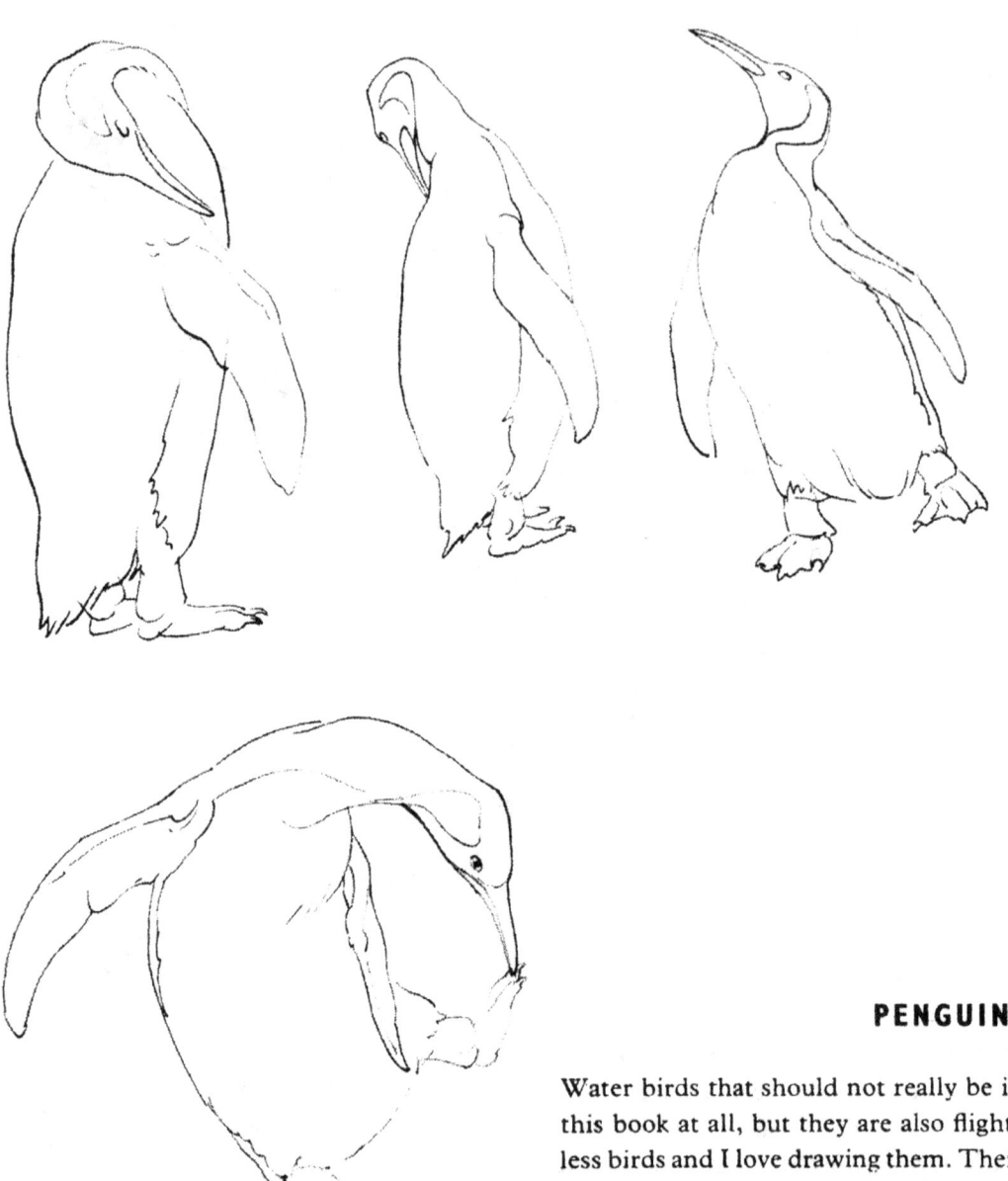

PENGUINS

Water birds that should not really be in this book at all, but they are also flightless birds and I love drawing them. Their wings have been modified as flippers and although they waddle in a most amusing

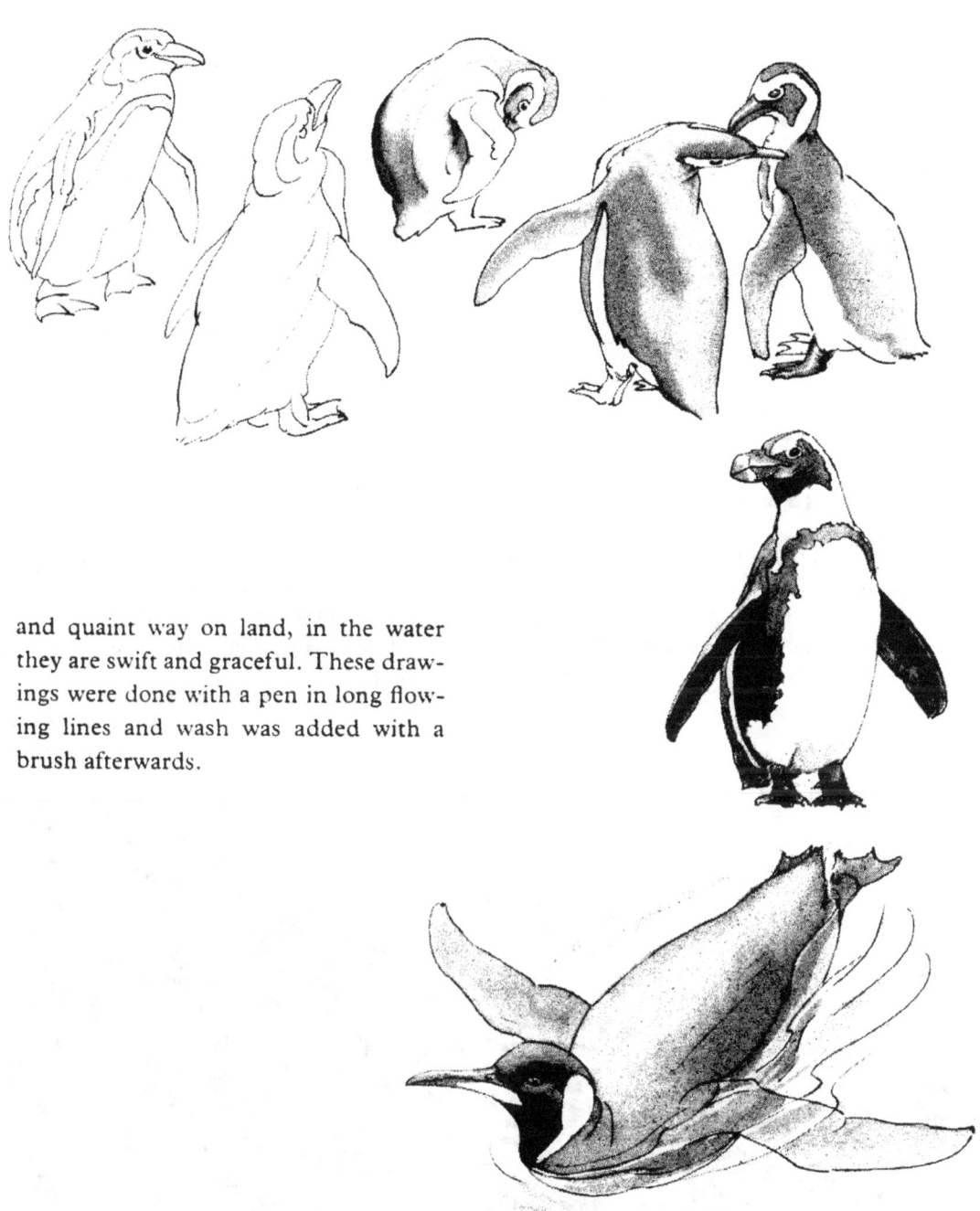

and quaint way on land, in the water
they are swift and graceful. These drawings were done with a pen in long flowing lines and wash was added with a
brush afterwards.

23

DRAWING WITH A BRUSH

The artists of ancient China and Japan always drew directly with a brush and its sensitive fluent tip is really the finest drawing instrument in the world. The small reproduction was drawn from life in colour. I just went for the main shapes and merely indicated the details. The larger, more finished drawing was done in prussian blue with a brush, but carried much further.

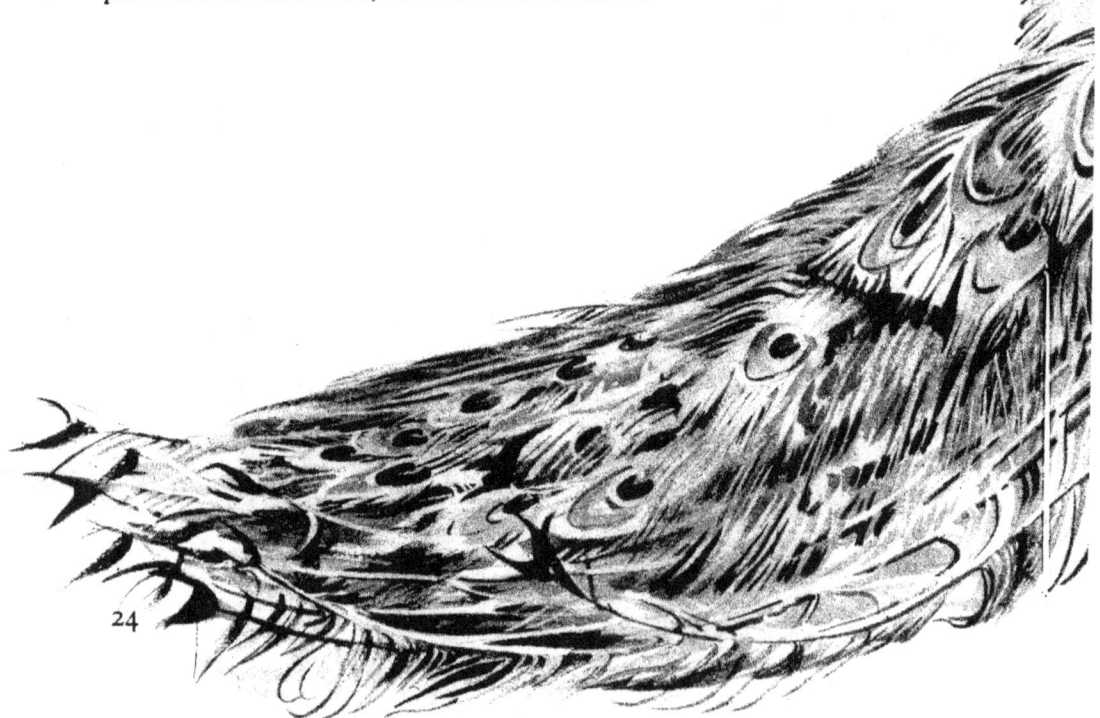

24

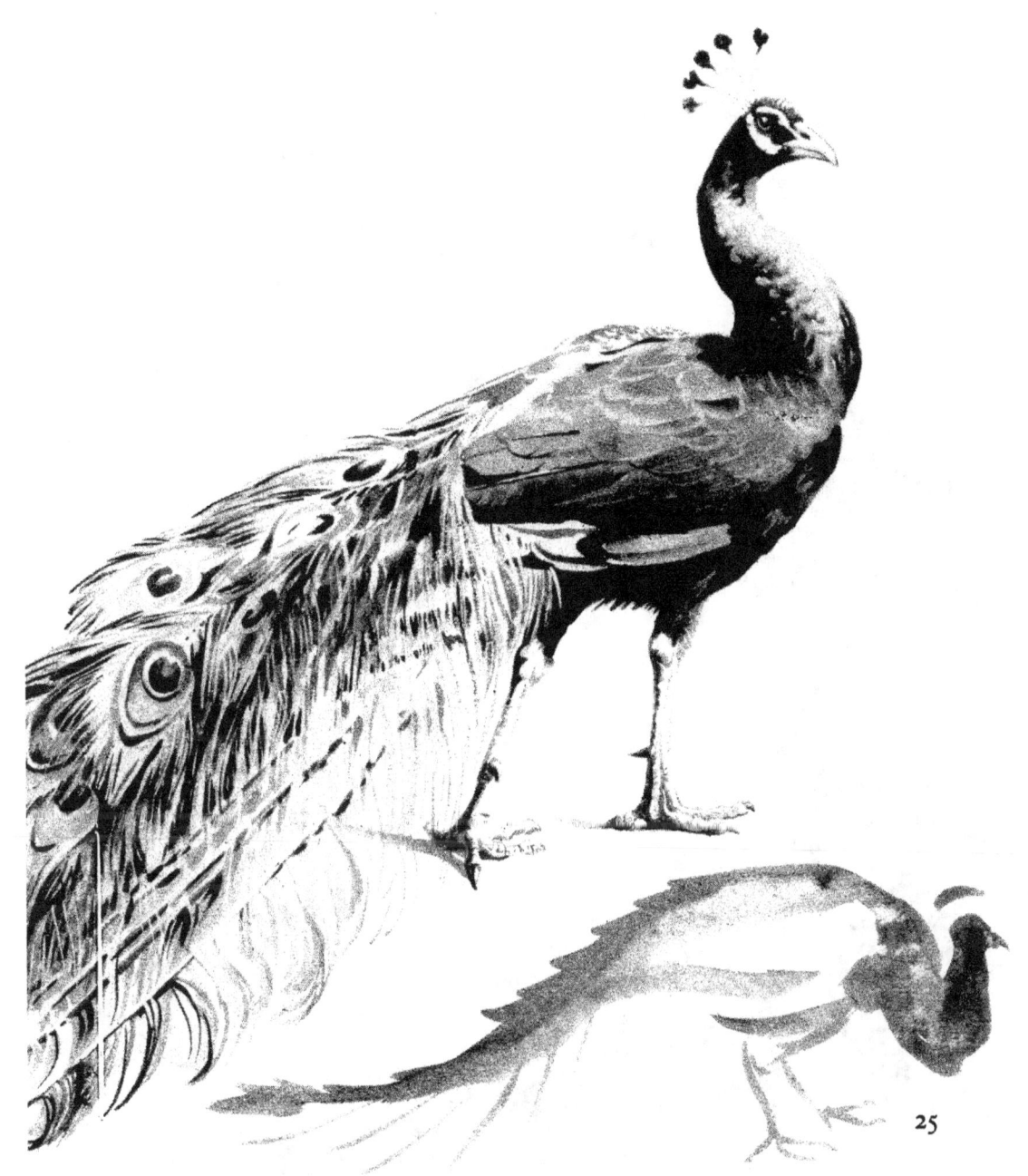

25

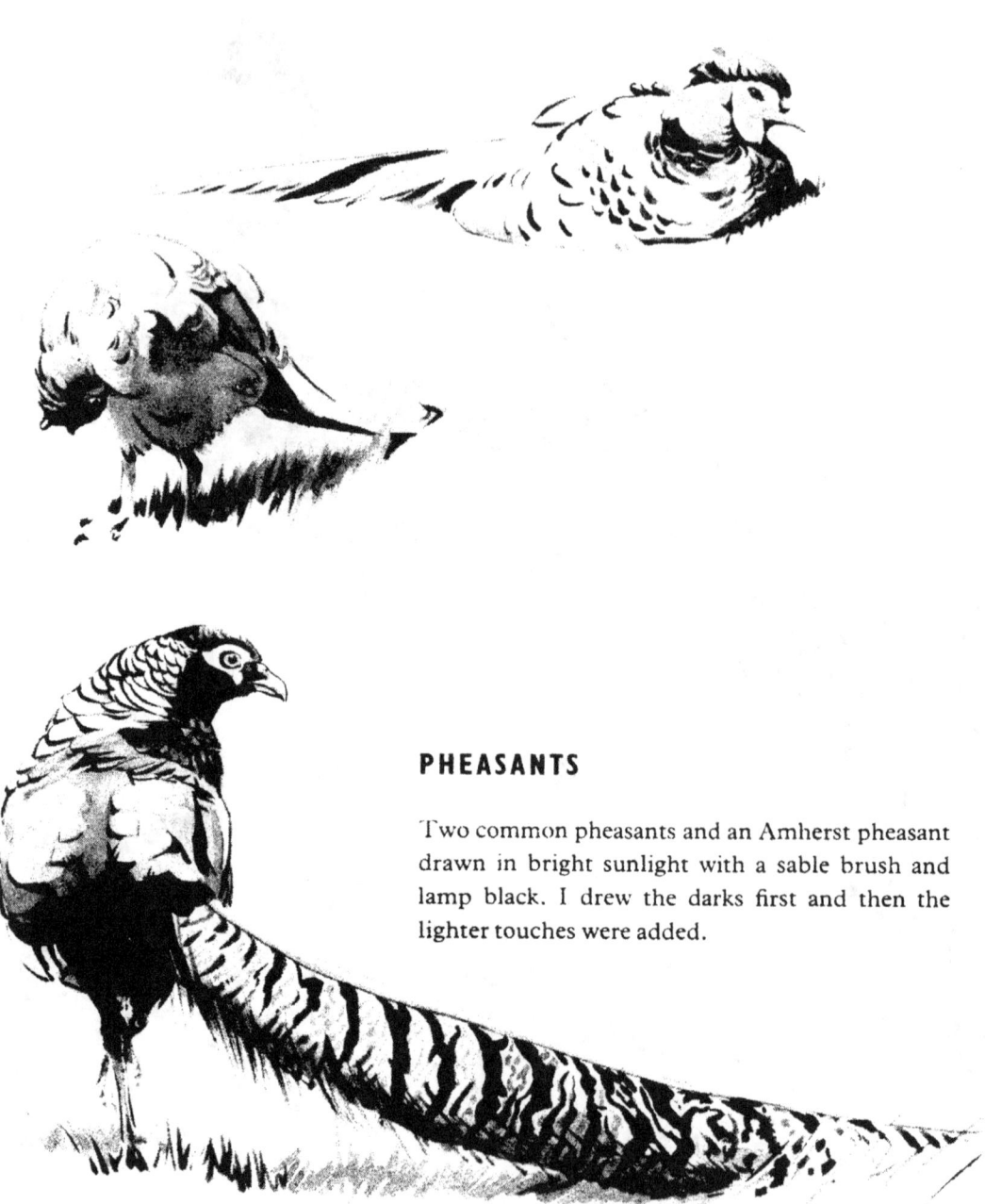

PHEASANTS

Two common pheasants and an Amherst pheasant drawn in bright sunlight with a sable brush and lamp black. I drew the darks first and then the lighter touches were added.

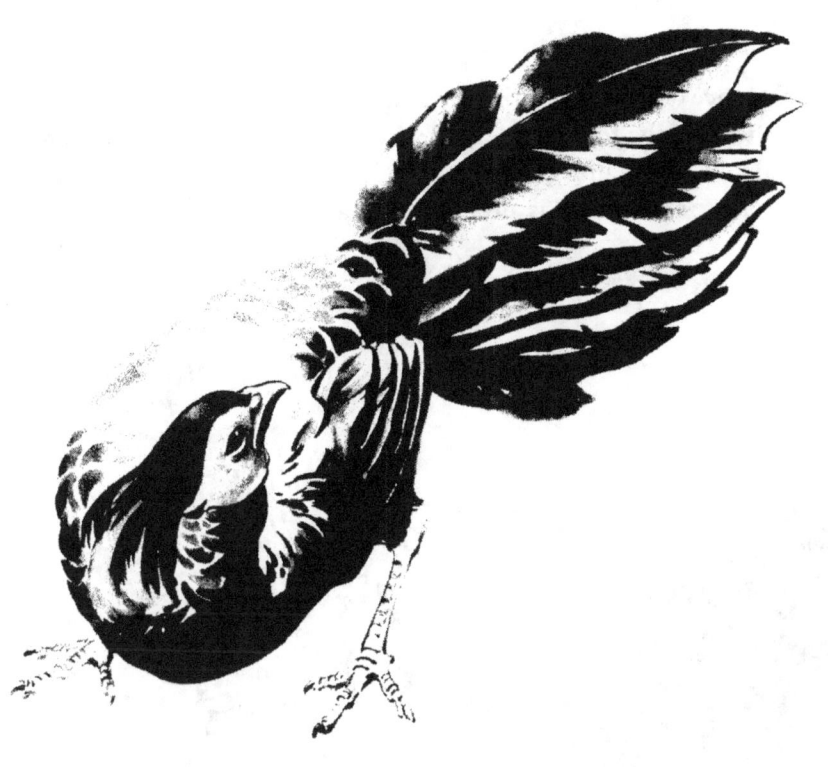

KALIJ PHEASANT

Although not as prettily marked as the Amherst I enjoy the fat strong shapes of his tail-feathers—a motif delicately repeated in feathers of the crest. The Kalij pheasant comes from India.

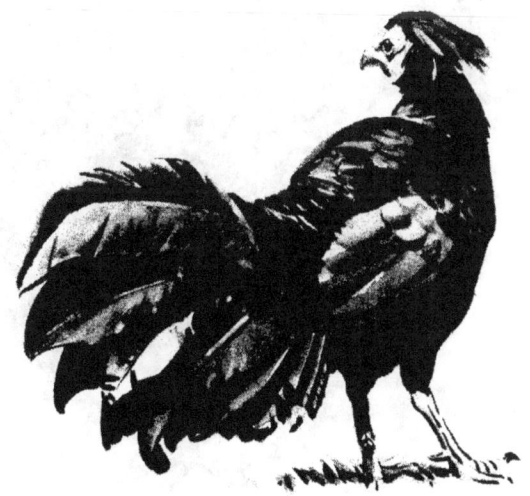

TURKEY

The familiar appearance of a turkey in display is shown below. The two outline drawings show: B, the form of the bird when its feathers lie naturally and A, how the back, flanks and mantle are erected and tail fanned out as, with half-opened wings, the entire appearance is altered and enlarged.

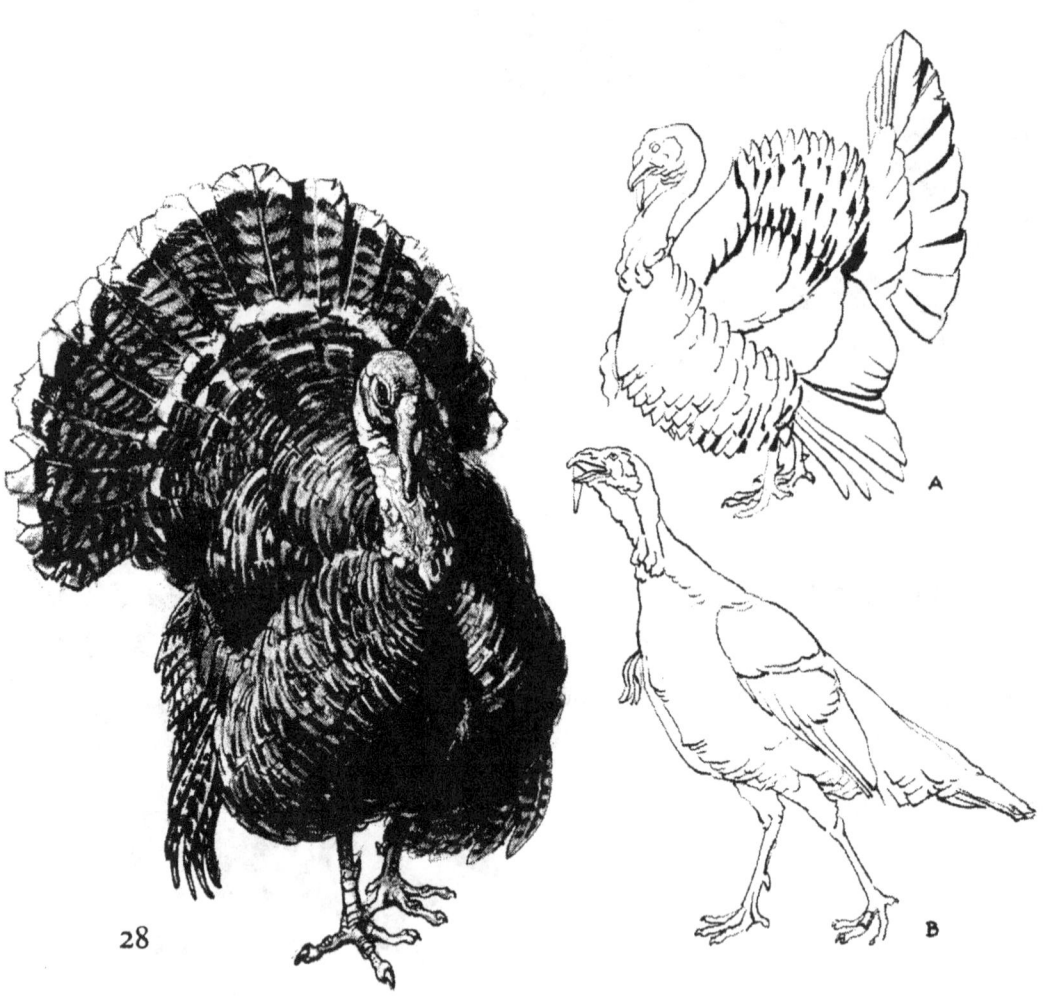

28

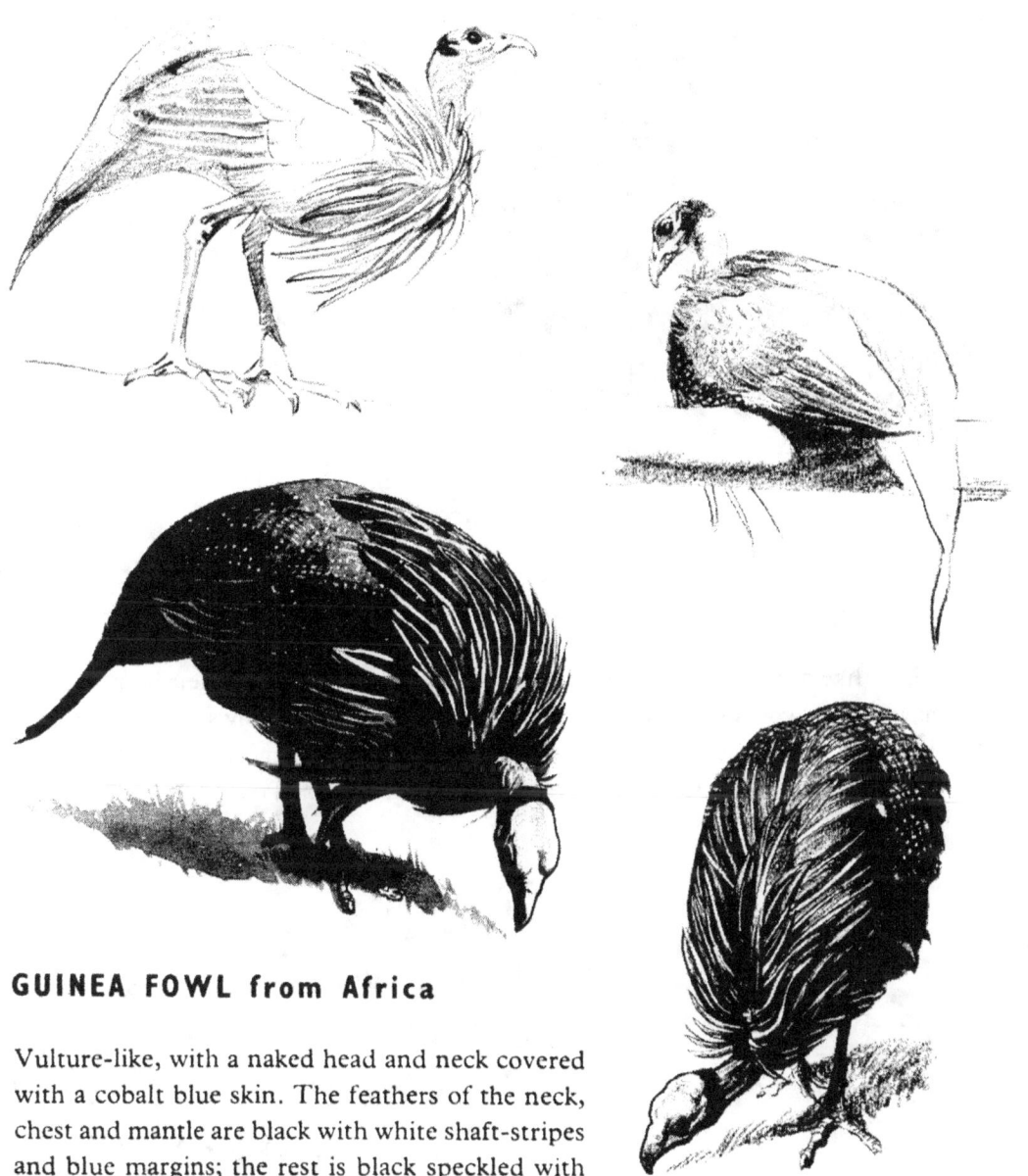

GUINEA FOWL from Africa

Vulture-like, with a naked head and neck covered with a cobalt blue skin. The feathers of the neck, chest and mantle are black with white shaft-stripes and blue margins; the rest is black speckled with white—the whole making a most handsomely marked bird.

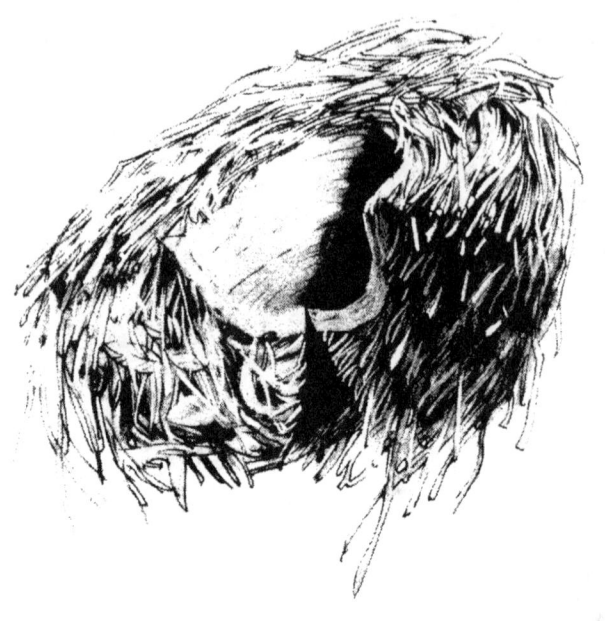

SOME NESTS
and how they are made

Birds, like ourselves, are builders, so here let us take a look at their homes. First I have shown you a section through a thrush's nest which shows the mud cup surrounded by straw and leaves. The chaffinch builds a delightful nest of moss and lichens lined with down or hair and it is generally in small trees like apple trees.

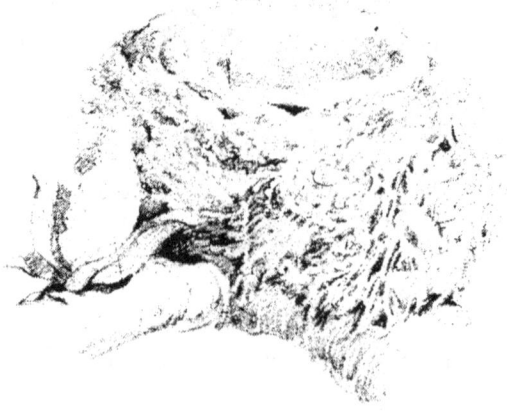

30

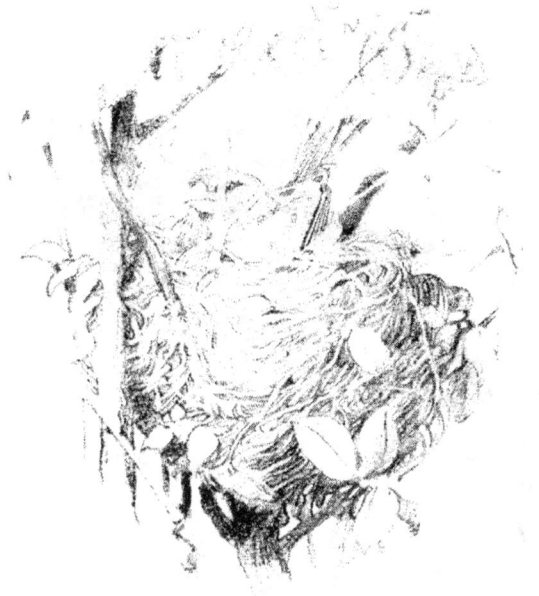

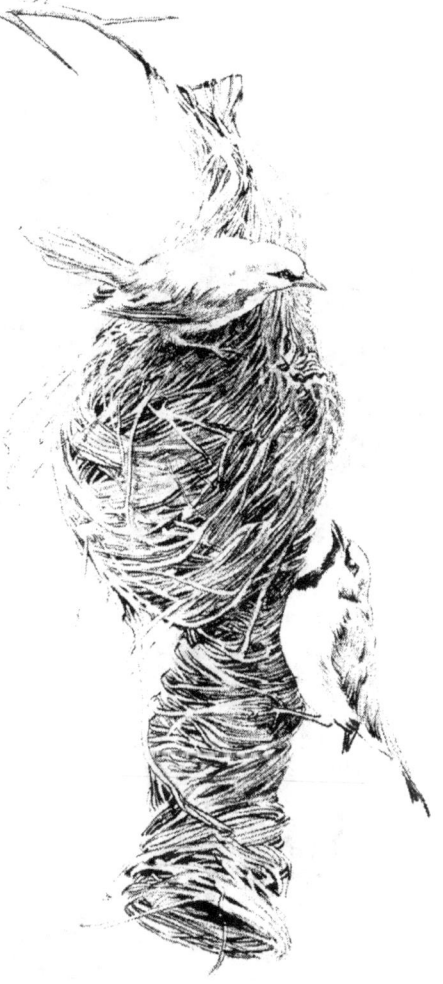

GREENFINCH

I peered through the leaves to draw this greenfinch who sat and watched me undismayed. It really was a fine chance to study a bird at close quarters. If you can discover a mother bird and do not get too close, you can draw for a long time.

WEAVER BIRDS

I drew the spectacled weaver birds on their nest from a model at the Natural History Museum, South Kensington. It is a wonderful structure made of dried grass woven into a ball with a cylindrical opening hanging down so that the eggs or young birds are quite safe from unwelcome intruders.

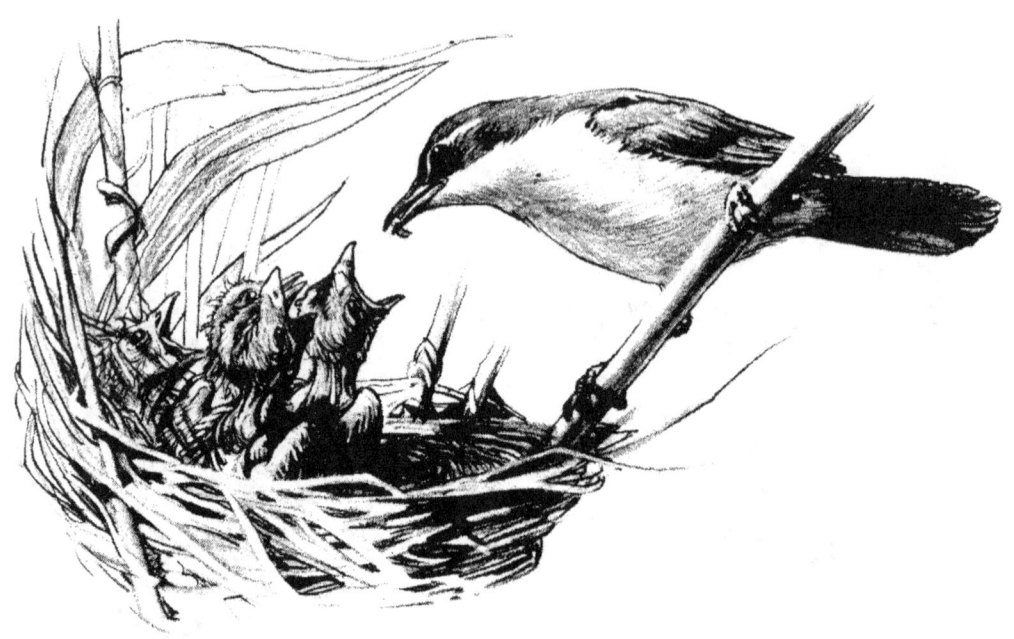

BABY BIRDS

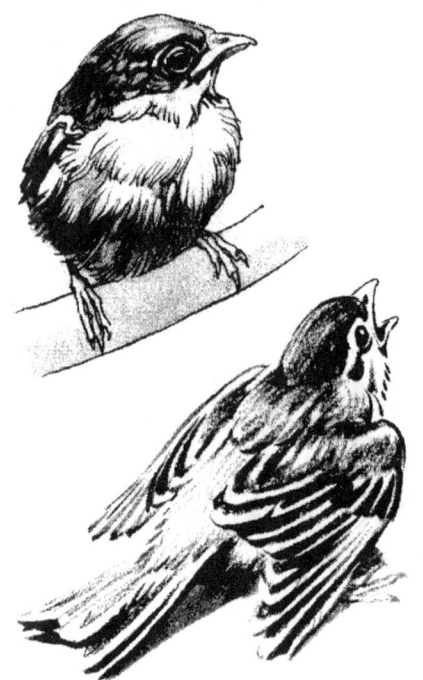

Baby birds grow very rapidly and indeed are soon fully fledged. The drawing at the top of this page shows some baby reed warblers only a few days old. Below is one fully fledged and a young sparrow just a little older. Look for the rather frog-like gape and the helpless flutterings of the half-open wings.

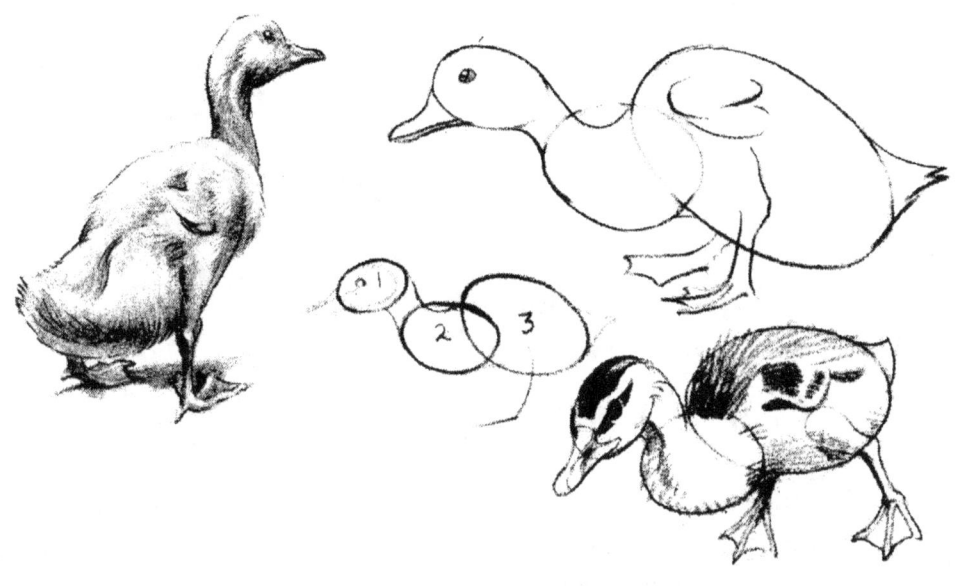

DOMESTIC DUCKLINGS
AND CHICKENS

Baby birds have a rounded form and a circle or oval can be a useful aid in building up its shape. Three over-lapping ovals help plan the relative position of head, chest and body of baby ducklings.

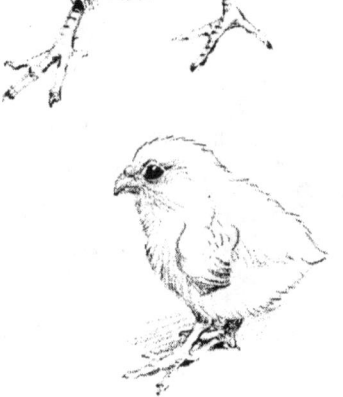

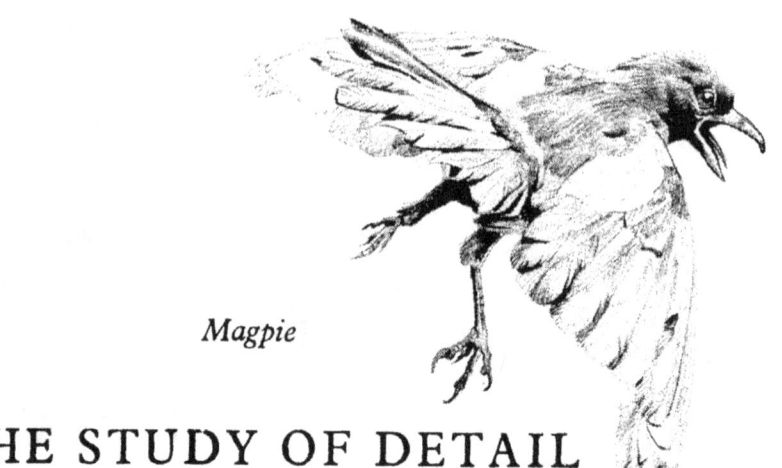

Magpie

THE STUDY OF DETAIL

SOMETIMES when the need is for information for a complete and accurate portrayal of a bird it is advisable to concentrate on some particular piece of detail; it may be the scales of the feet, the fore-shortening of a folded wing or some particular view-point of the head. It is, of course, a great help if one can get hold of a dead specimen for this kind of study. I have made many such useful drawings from dead birds: unfortunate

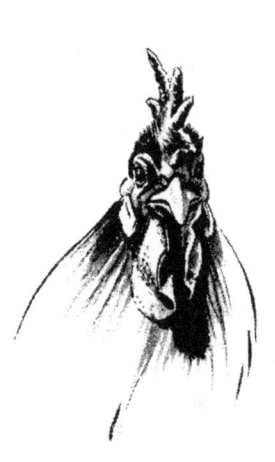

fledgelings that have fallen from the nests, as well as adult specimens. It is extremely useful too, to make very careful drawings from the well mounted specimens in a museum of Natural History. This is particularly helpful when studying a bird with strongly patterned plumage. One is able to concentrate on it as a piece of still life. This sort of drawing should never be considered a substitute for drawing from the live bird, but merely as a means of increasing knowledge and clarifying difficulties. Studies made from a bird mounted in an attitude of flight are a great aid towards mastering the difficulties of drawing foreshortened wings and tails.

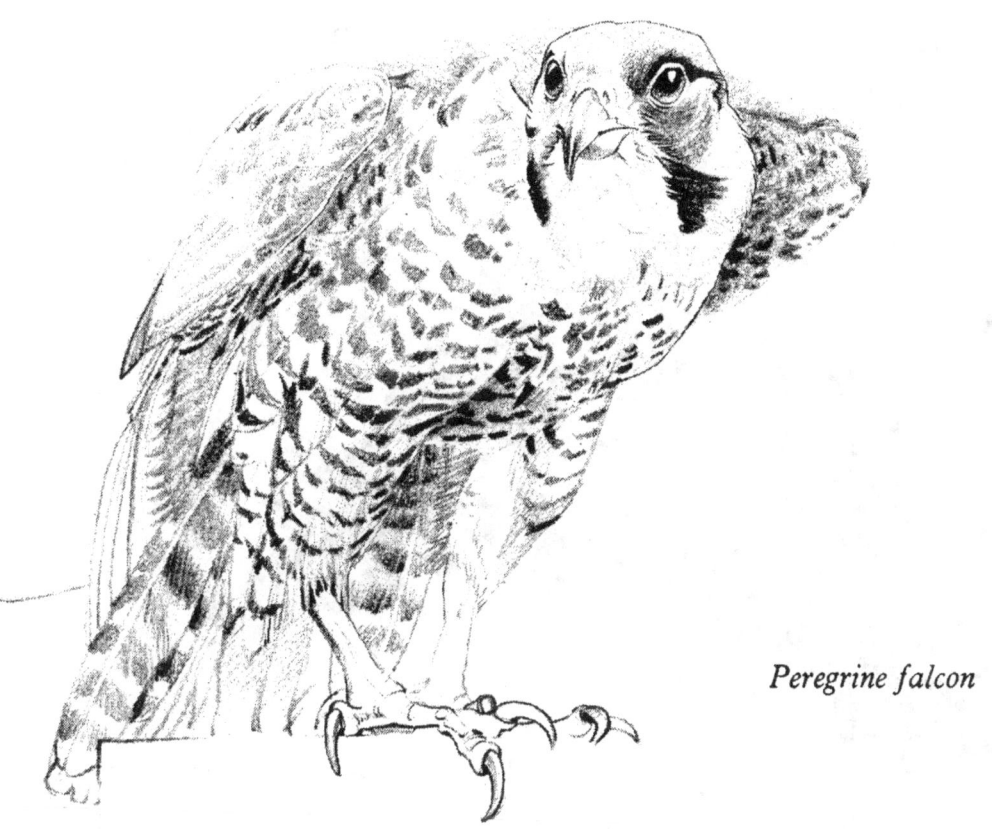

Peregrine falcon

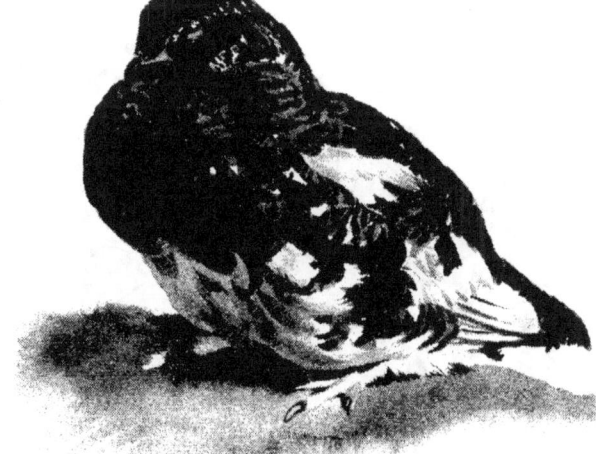

Ptarmigan

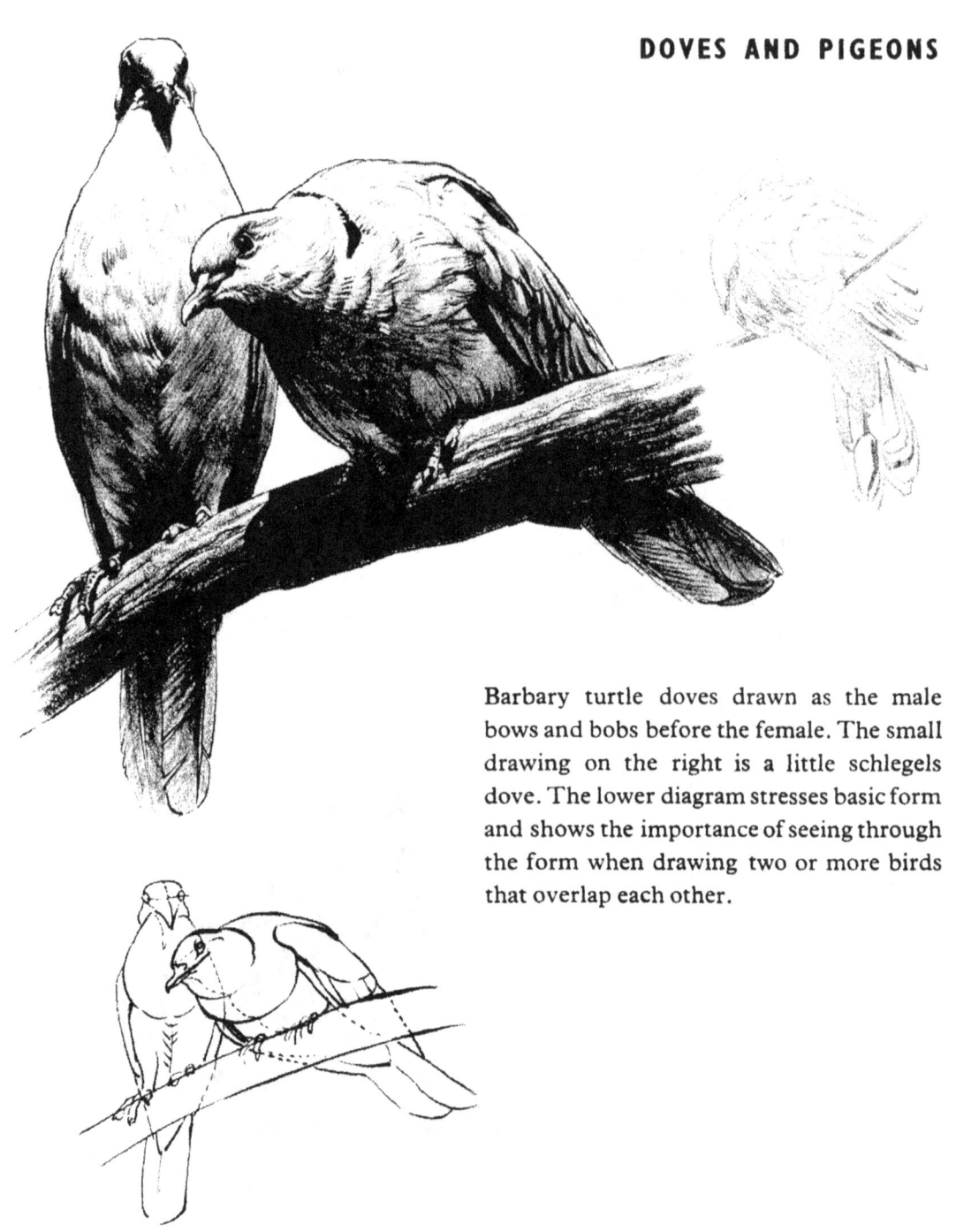

Barbary turtle doves drawn as the male bows and bobs before the female. The small drawing on the right is a little schlegels dove. The lower diagram stresses basic form and shows the importance of seeing through the form when drawing two or more birds that overlap each other.

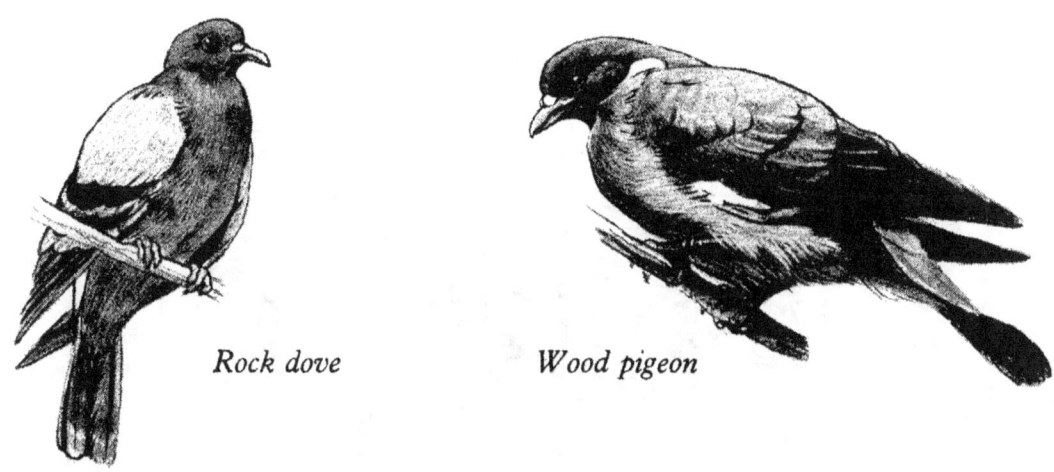

Rock dove   *Wood pigeon*

This white domestic pigeon proudly parading on the ground is descended, as are all domestic pigeons, from the rock dove (upper left). They should not be confused with the much more common wood-pigeon or ring-dove, shown here for purposes of comparison.

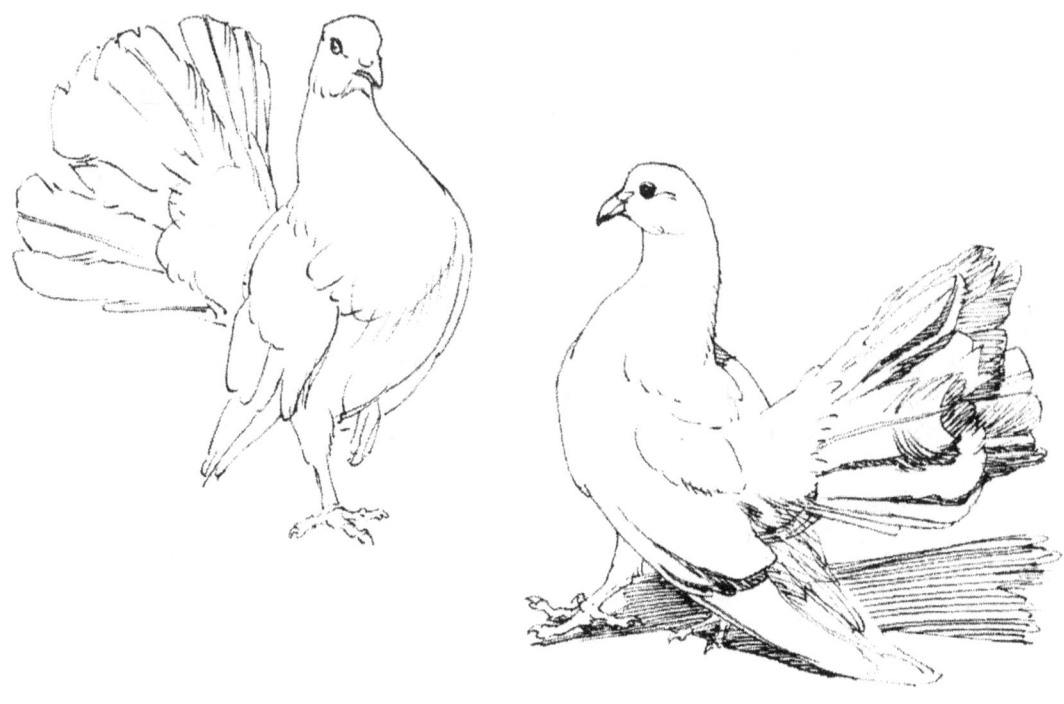

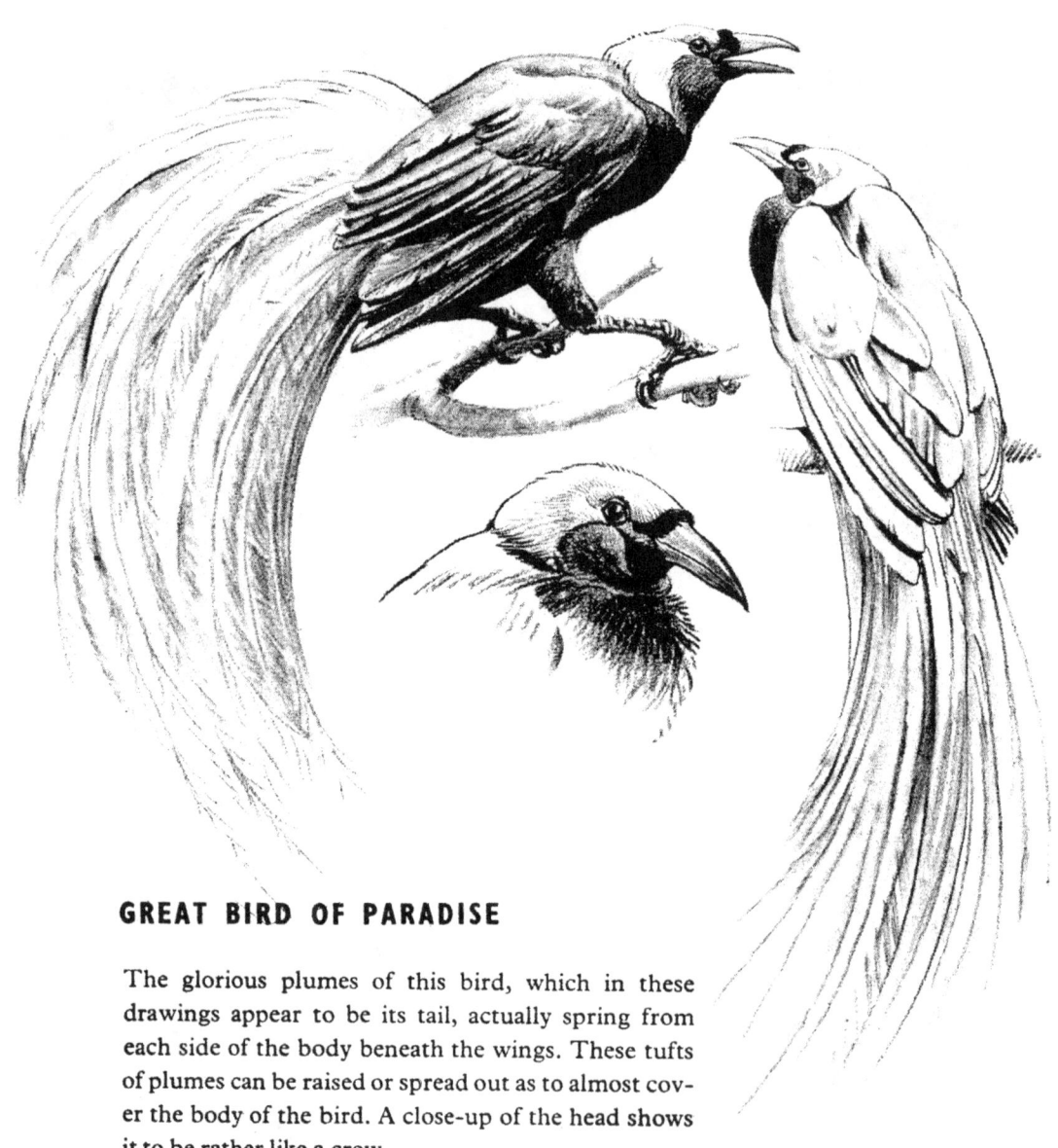

GREAT BIRD OF PARADISE

The glorious plumes of this bird, which in these drawings appear to be its tail, actually spring from each side of the body beneath the wings. These tufts of plumes can be raised or spread out as to almost cover the body of the bird. A close-up of the head shows it to be rather like a crow.

38

AUSTRALIAN LYRE BIRD

This is, to the artist, a most decorative bird. The extraordinary lyrate shaped tail feathers of the male bird are lovely even when the bird is just perching on a branch as shown here, but most beautiful when thrown forward over the crouched body in the full glory of display.

Overleaf I have drawn the bird in full display on a piece of black scraperboard. The white lines are scraped away with a special nib. I chose this method because it gives the delicate feathery effect so necessary in depicting the plumes of the bird.

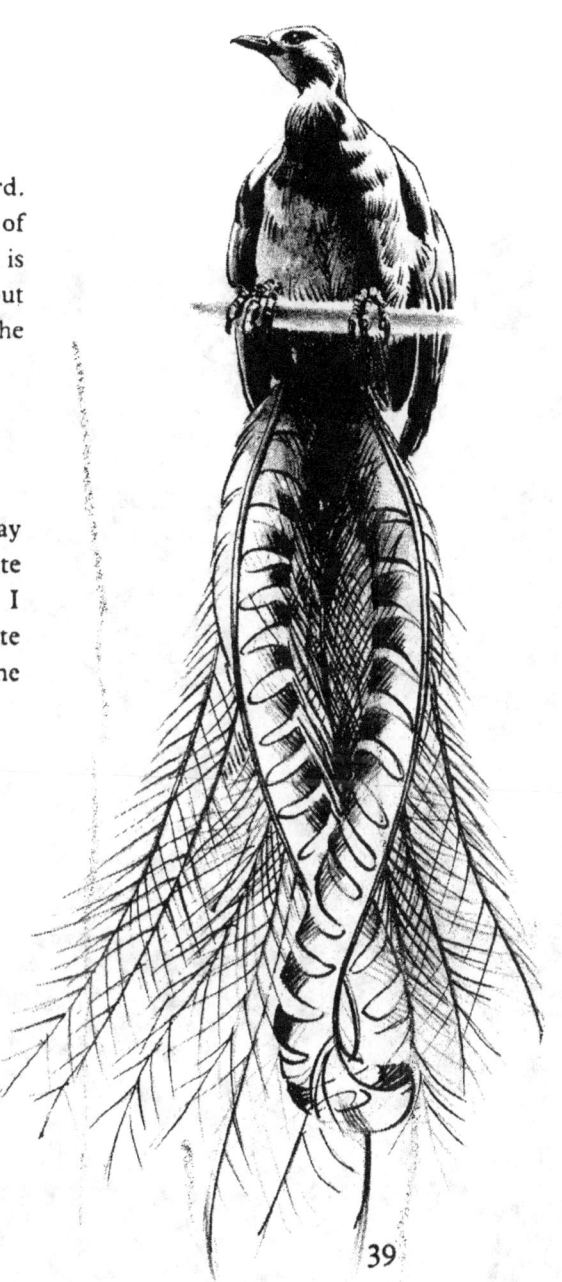

39

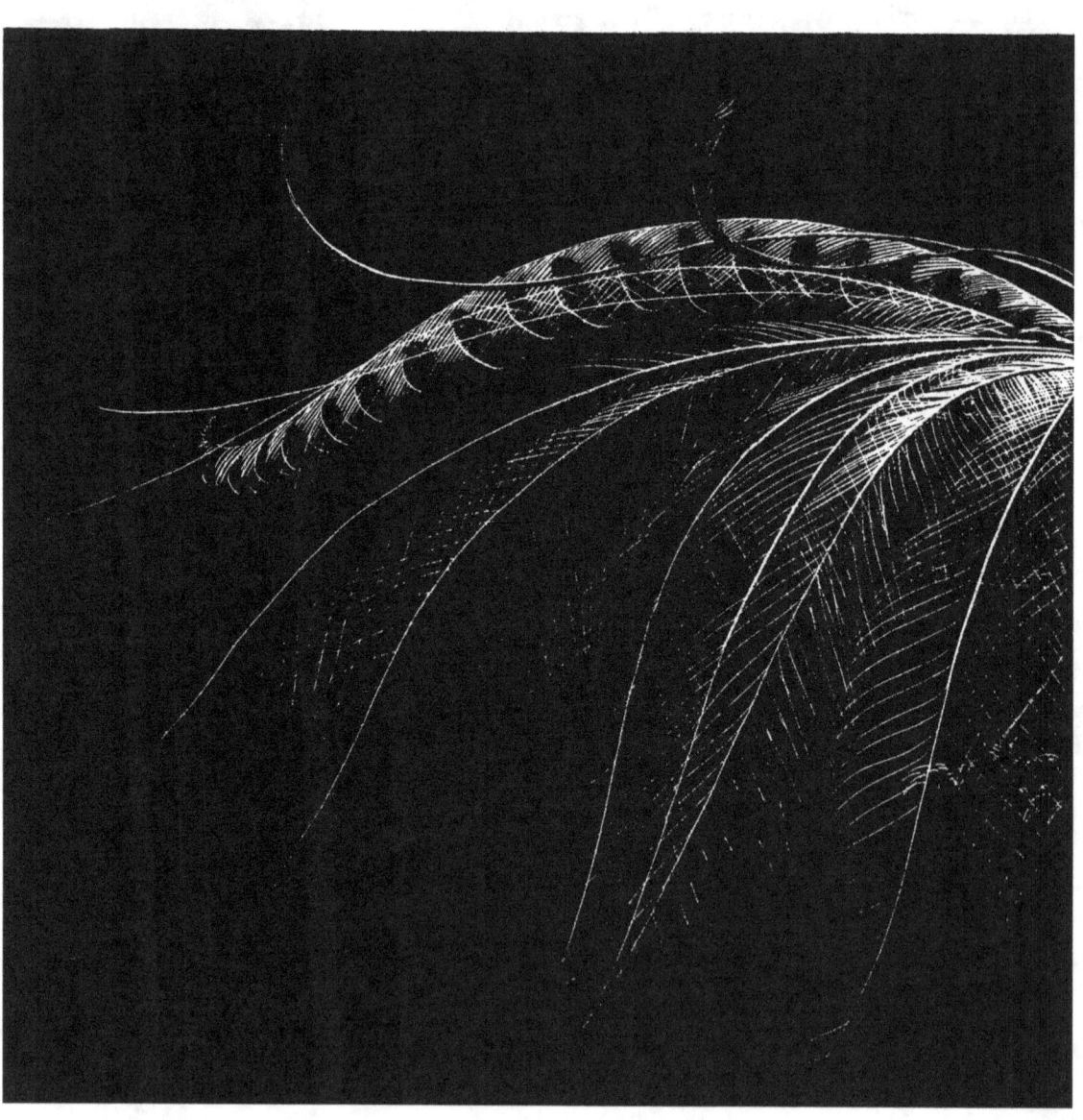

AUSTRALIAN LYRE BIRD

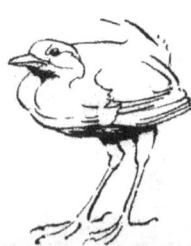

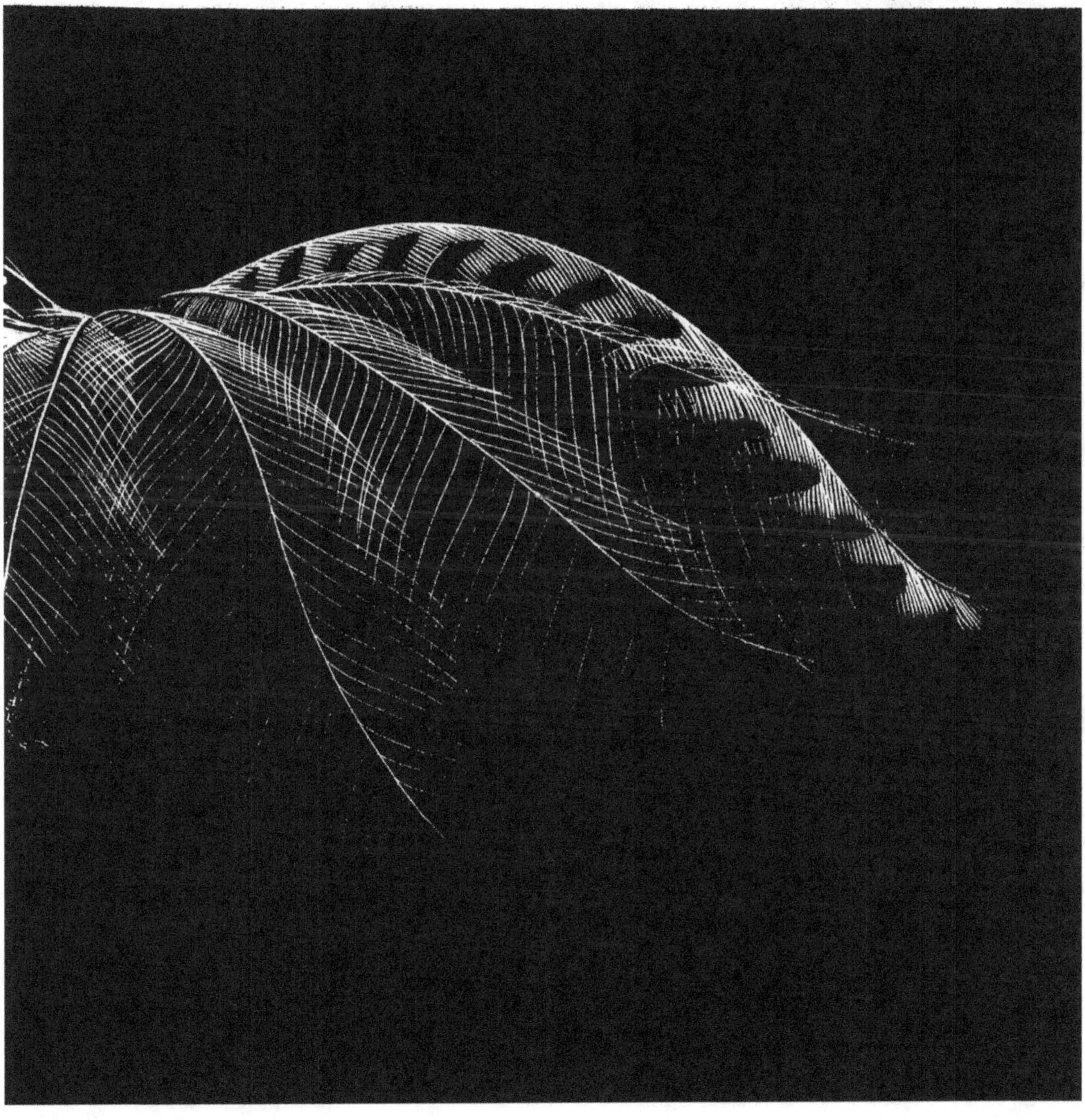

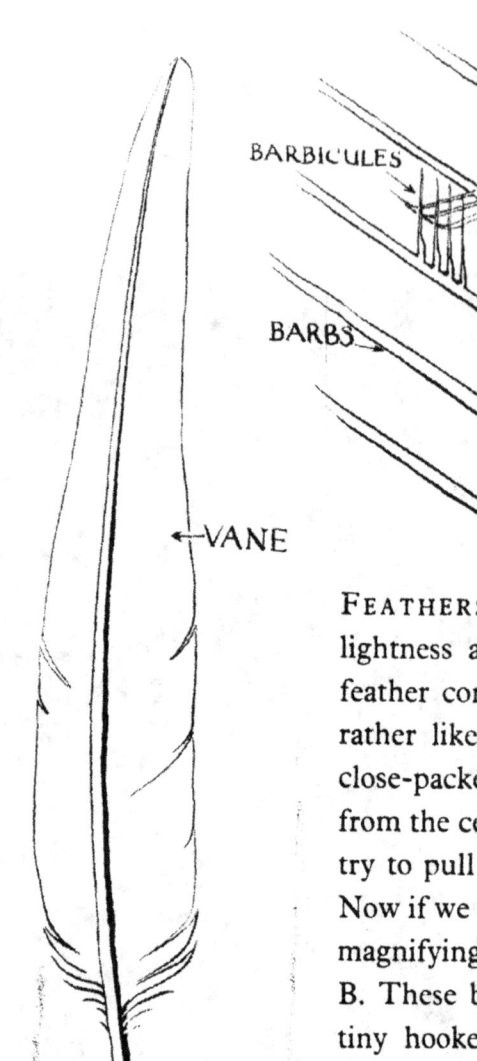

BARBICULES

BARBS

VANE

SHAFT

B

HOW BIRDS FLY

FEATHERS make flight possible. They are a marvel of lightness and flexibility combined with strength. A feather consists of a stiff central shaft and a vane— rather like a windmill. The vane consists of many close-packed minor shafts growing out at an angle from the central one. These are called barbs and if we try to pull them apart they appear to cling together. Now if we were to examine a section under a powerful magnifying glass we would see something like diagram B. These barbs are held together by a criss-cross of tiny hooked barbicules. The whole vane is thus a strong air-resistant surface.

The feathers on a bird's wing are grouped together in such a way that a section through the wing would look like the black shape in the diagrams opposite.

When the wing moves forward through the air a strong suction or lift is created over the upper surface of the wing—strong enough to overcome both gravity and the downward pull of the slighter suction below. This lift is increased if the wing is tilted back further, B, but a point is soon reached when too much tilt would break up the air-flow on the upper surface and cause the bird to stall, C. However, by thrusting forward a small group of feathers called the alulae, the bird can increase the air-flow across the upper surface and thus restore balance, D.

The lower diagrams show a section through the flight feathers and how they can rotate in order to let air pass between them on the upthrust and

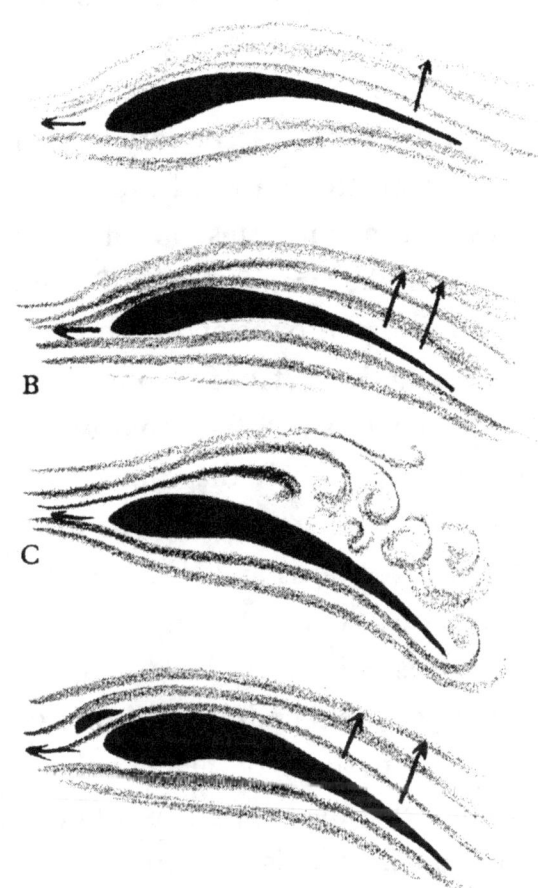

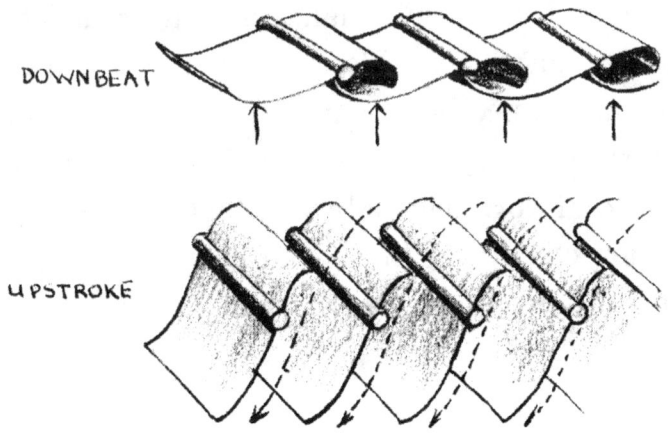

DOWNBEAT

UPSTROKE

43

how the downthrust causes them to lock together.

In flight the bird actually propels itself through the air by its primary feathers, the outer section of its wing (which corresponds anatomically to our hand). The secondary feathers and coverts on the inner part of the wing (arm) are cambered and hollowed as the section shown on the previous page, and it is this part of the wing that maintains the 'lift'.

Birds, like aircraft, take off into the wind. Some, with powerful legs, run or jump into the air accompanied by violent wing-beats; water birds taxi along the surface for some distance before rising; whilst weak legged birds like the swifts have to drop from a high ledge or cliff in order to get flying speed. These diagrams show how the bird beats downwards with its flight feathers closed, but how they gradually open as the wing is brought forwards and then completely so in the last one as the wing is drawn up again.

This is only a very brief and bare account of the mechanics of flight, but it does help to draw birds in flight if this mechanism is understood.

The wing-beats of the hovering humming-bird are so rapid that, to the human eye, they appear as a faint blur around a small body apparently suspended on invisible wires. Now this is the extreme of such movement in the bird world but it is a fact that, in rapid flight, the wing-beats of a small bird such as a sparrow register a double impression on the eye, which appears to see, at the same time, the extremes of the upstroke and the down-beat with the intervening stages a faint blur. However, this is not a very satisfactory method of portraying a bird in flight. There is a slight pause at the completion of both up and down beats, also, birds hold their wings still, sometimes half-shut, as they glide or swoop be-

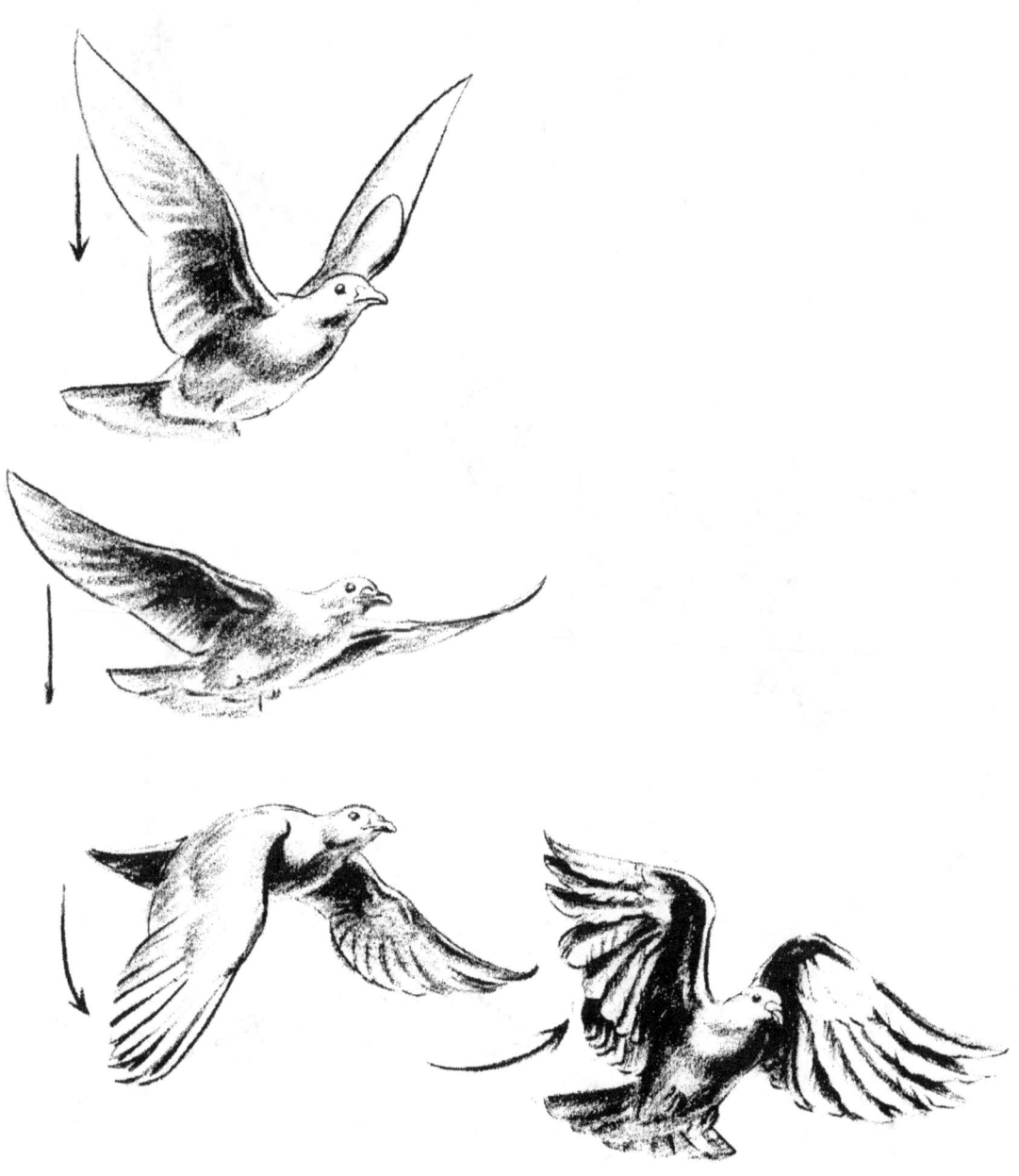

tween moments of flying. Close observation will tell you which is the best attitude for a particular species. Avoid the attitude which looks like a cross (diagram A) as this gives a static effect— one line opposing the direction of the other. If that position of the wings is unavoidable draw them in perspective (as in diagram B) and try to emphasise the arrow-shape formed by the leading edges and head of the bird, this will give an impression of forward movement.

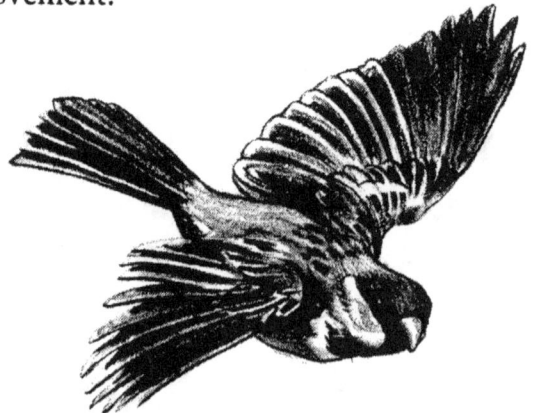

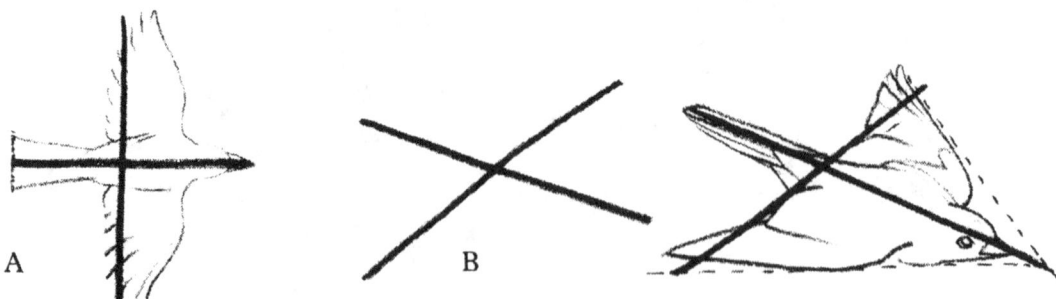

A

B

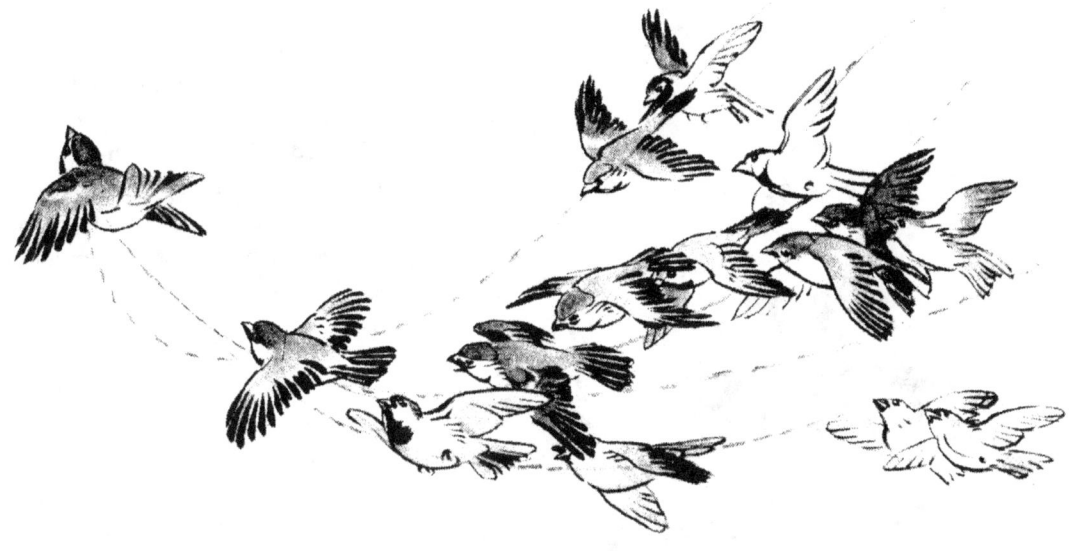

It is great fun looking at flocks of birds in flight. Pigeons, starlings and sparrows can be seen everywhere. The Japanese artists who produced such lively colour prints during the eighteenth and nineteenth centuries were masters at drawing groups of flying birds. Notice how some of the birds appear massed together as one bird overlaps another. The fluttering flight of a flock of sparrows can best be suggested by arranging them in such a way that they form a slightly rising and falling line. The drawing here reproduced is based on a Japanese print of the early nineteenth century and I think it shows very well both the character of the bird's flight and the underlying rhythmic lines of the whole design which, by their convergence, emphasize the forward movement.

Each species has its distinctive flight; from the woodpecker, switchbacking up and down to the zig-zag movement of a snipe. Observation of such characteristics will make your drawings so much more truthful.

DRAWING AT A ROOKERY

Who has not stood under great elm trees in March as the wind roars through the branches, admiring the way the rooks build their great nests? I used a fountain pen and smudged with my finger to get the effect down rapidly. The close-ups of the birds were drawn with the same medium but touched up with a wash of lamp-black water colour afterwards.

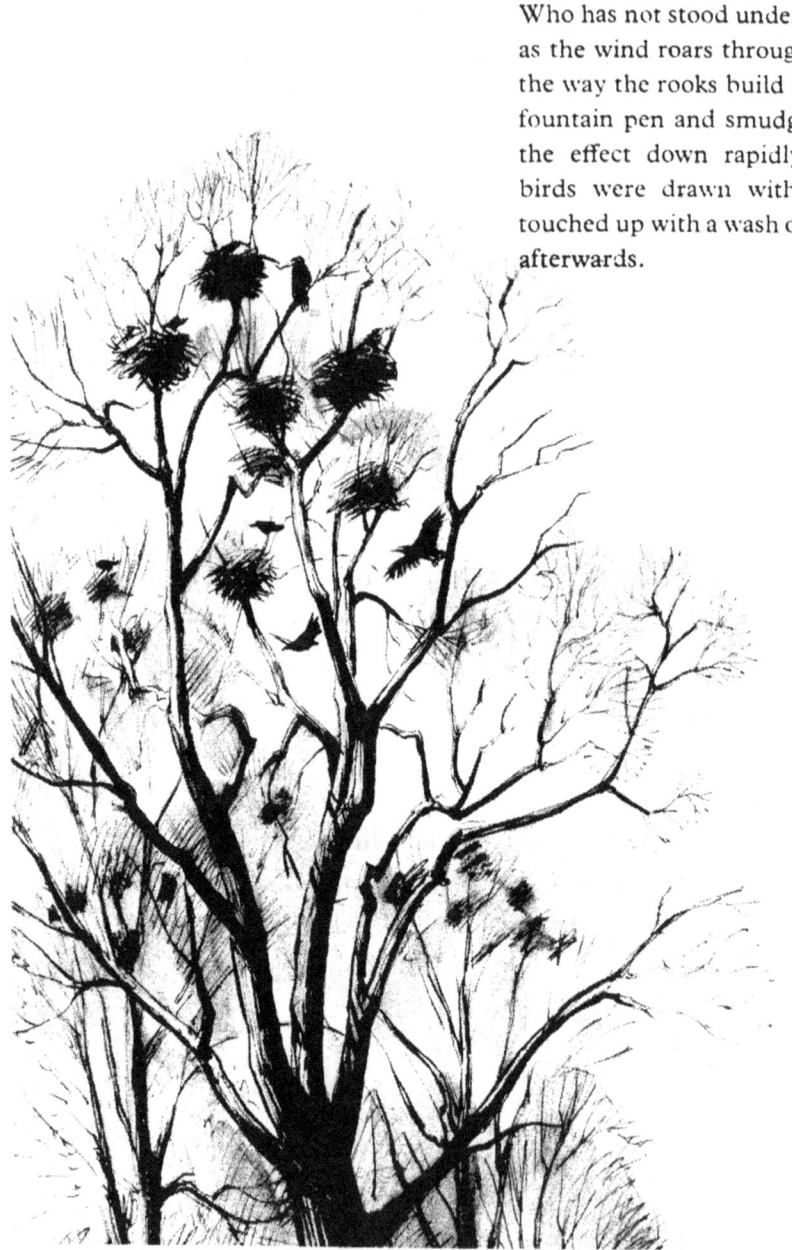

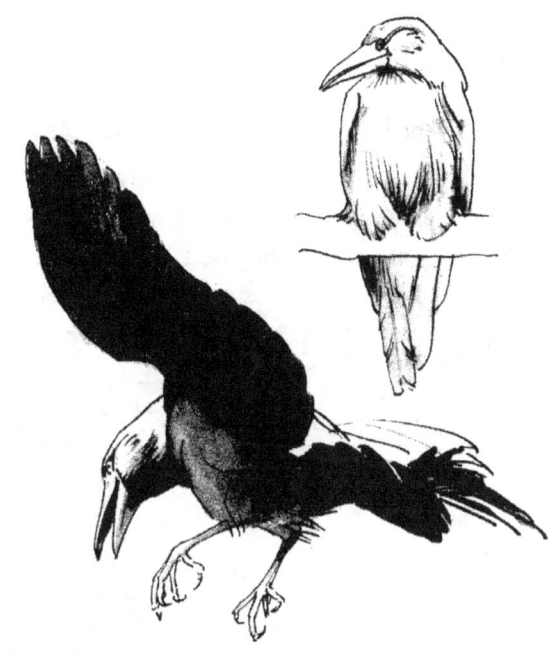

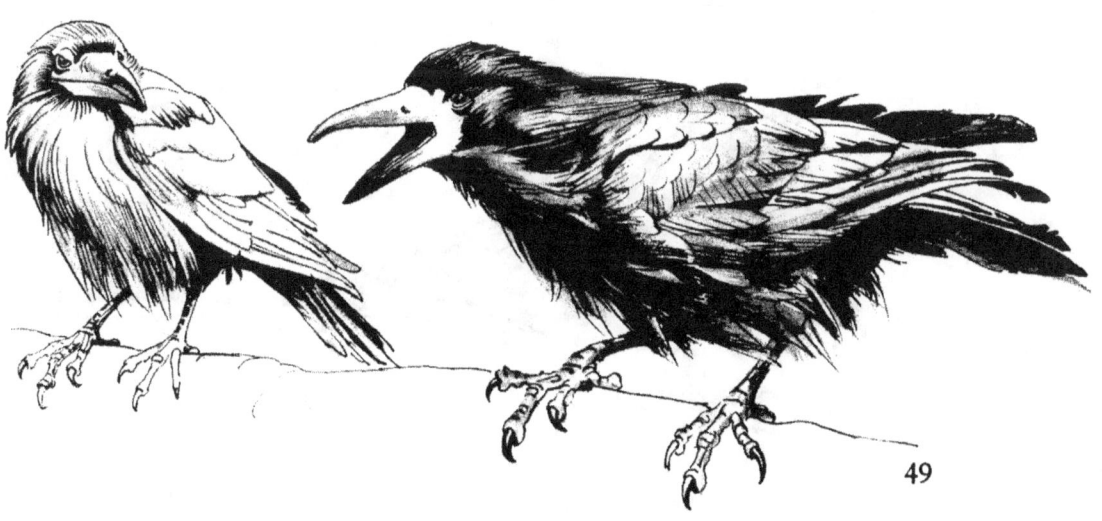

49

MAGPIES

This bird kept still with its wings not quite shut until I had completed it. I drew it afterwards in outline with a carbon pencil, as it hopped about the ground. These outlines were then fused and softened with a stump of soft paper.

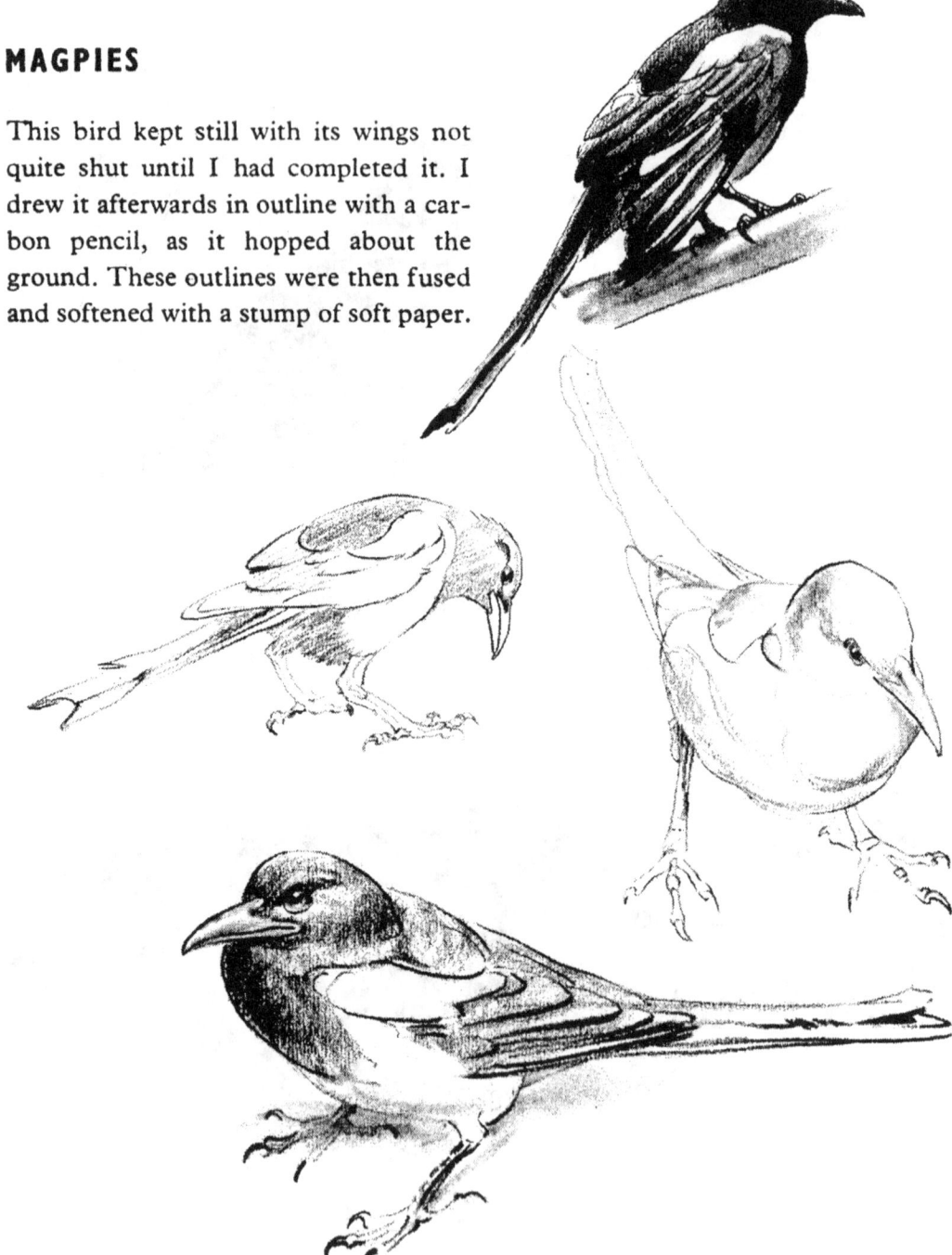

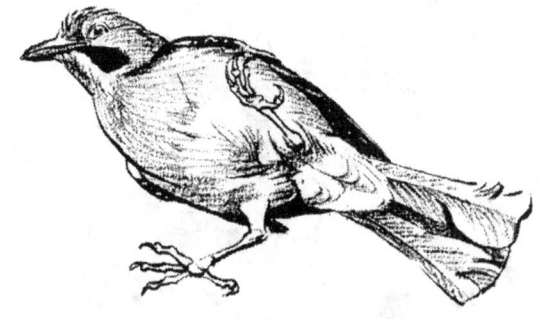

JAYS

This bird in an aviary flew backwards and forwards and I was able to make a study of its flying attitude as it came in to land.

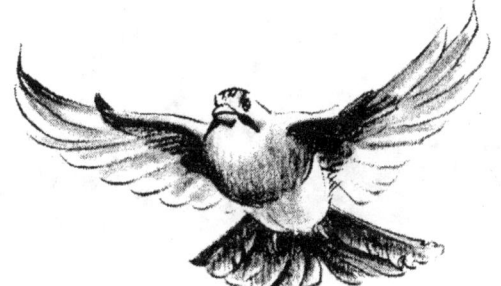

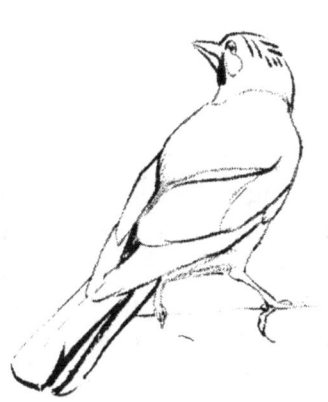

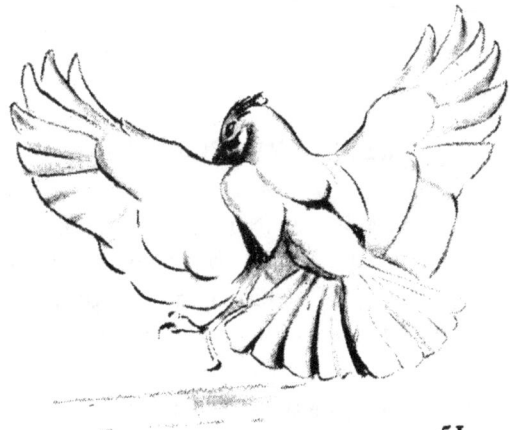

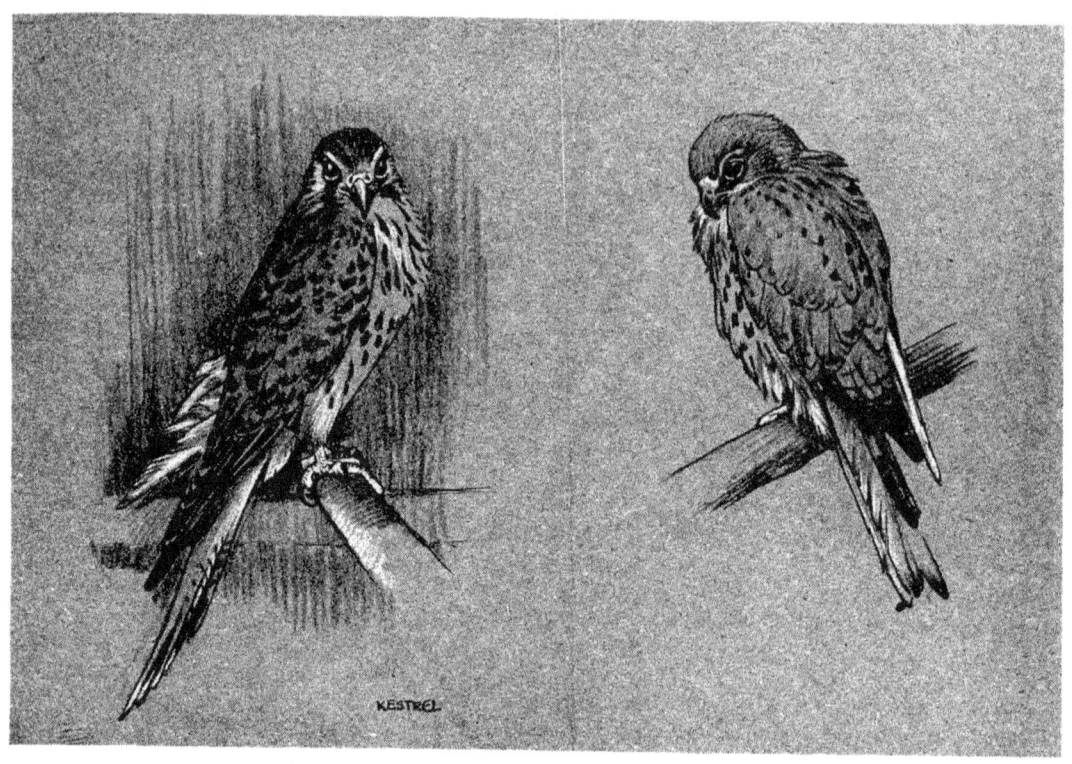

KESTREL

KESTRELS AND CONDORS

These studies were made on ordinary brown wrapping paper which gives a nice middle tone. I used a black conté crayon with white for the lights. This is a very useful way of making complete tone studies and is also a great help in bright sunlight when white paper has an unpleasant glare. Both these birds sat very still although I seized the opportunity to make a note as the condor stretched its wings in characteristic attitude.

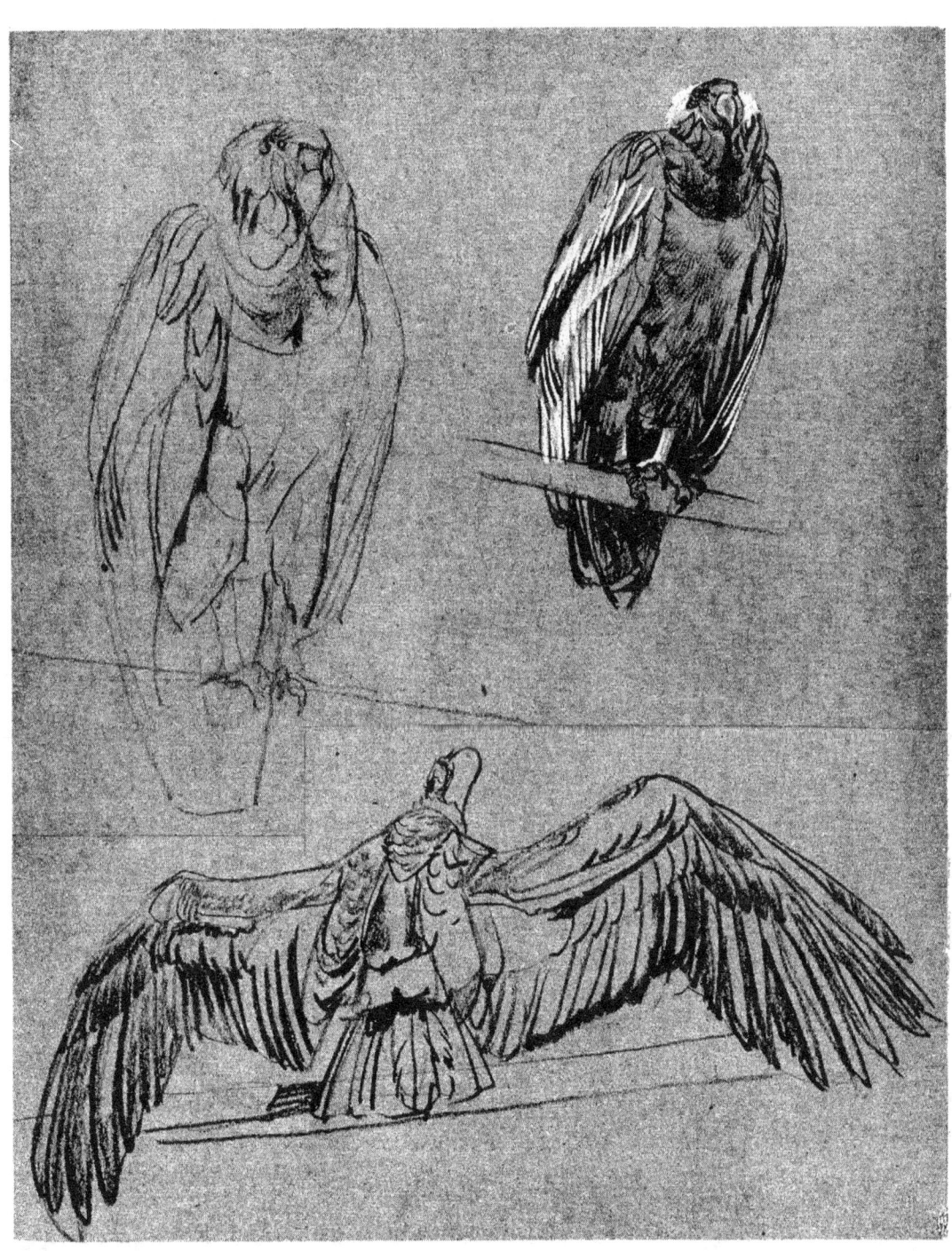

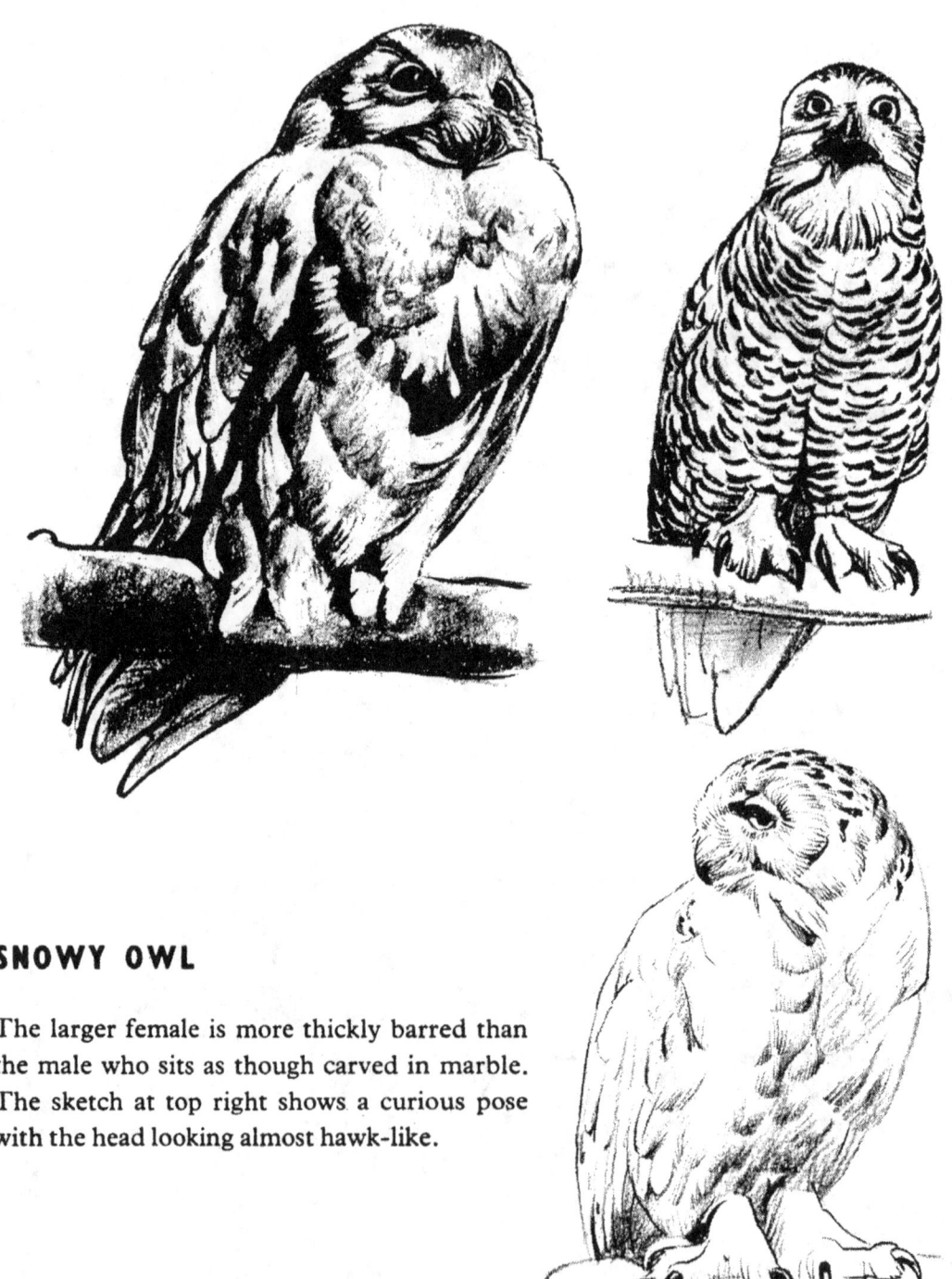

SNOWY OWL

The larger female is more thickly barred than the male who sits as though carved in marble. The sketch at top right shows a curious pose with the head looking almost hawk-like.

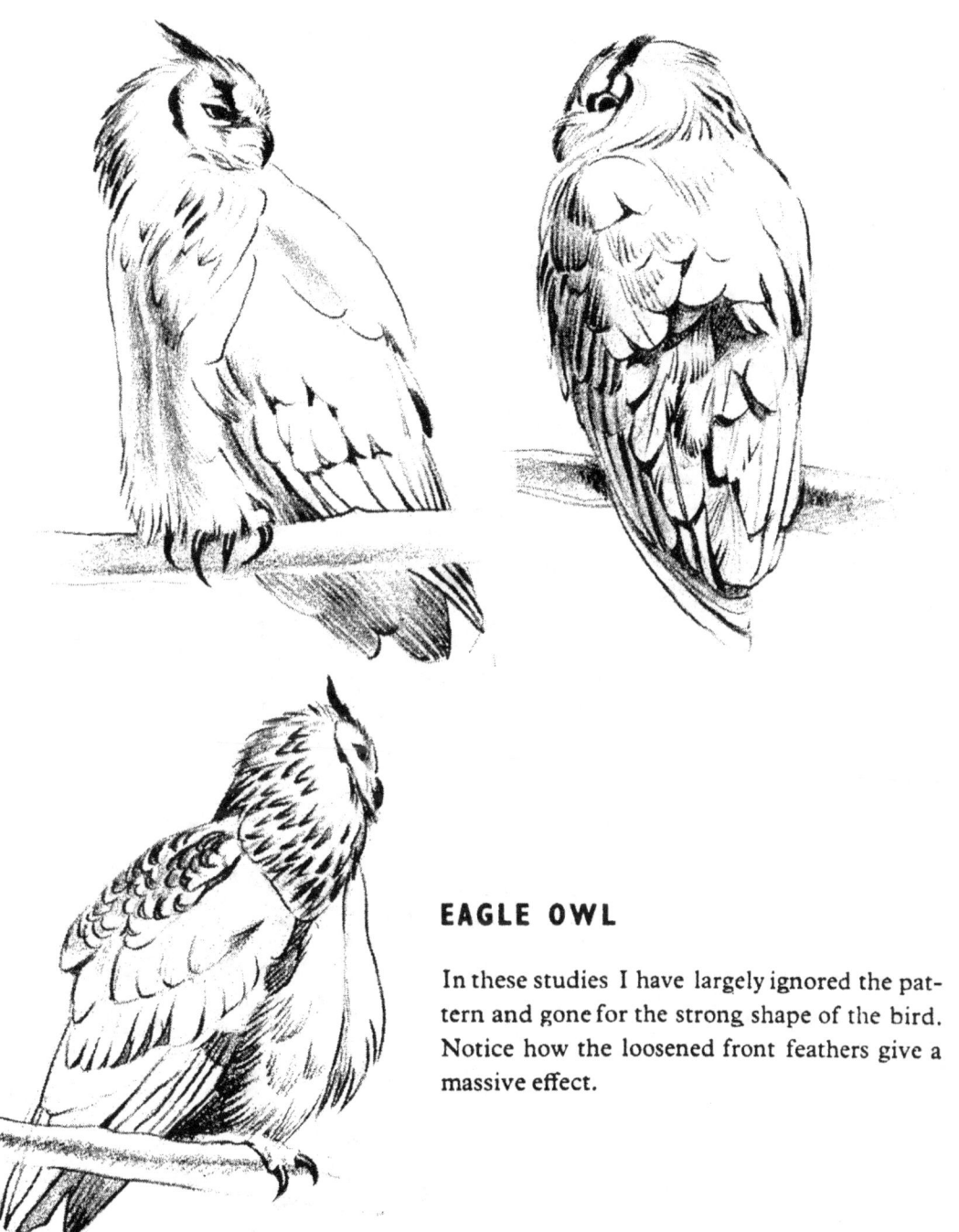

EAGLE OWL

In these studies I have largely ignored the pattern and gone for the strong shape of the bird. Notice how the loosened front feathers give a massive effect.

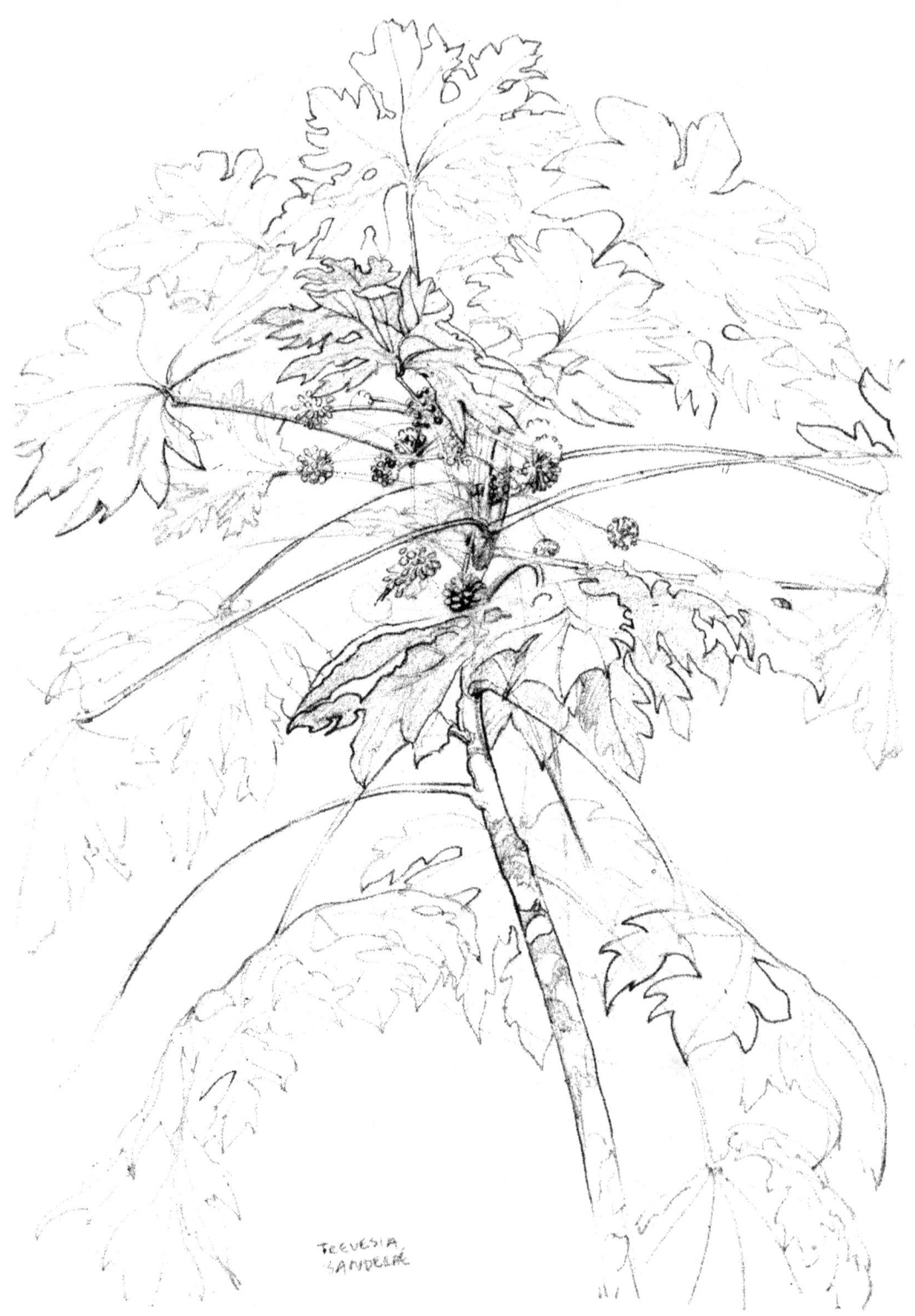

TREVESIA
SANDERII

BACKGROUND STUDIES

On this page are two drawings I made from nature to be used as background for bird pictures. They are included here because it is important to make many such studies in preparation for the time later on when you wish to depict birds in a natural setting. The pencil drawing on the left was done in the Palm House at Kew Gardens. The rhododendrons were done out of doors in line and water colour.

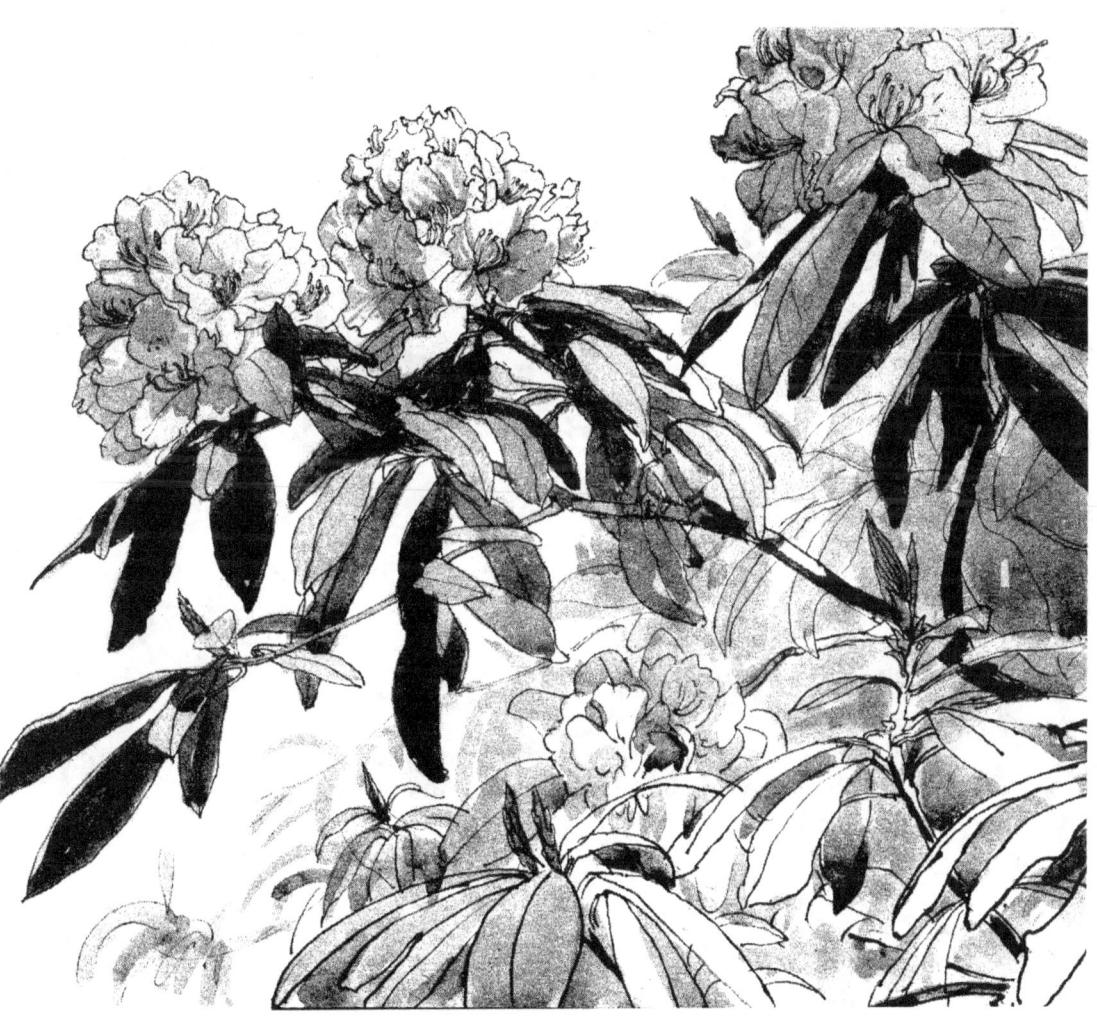

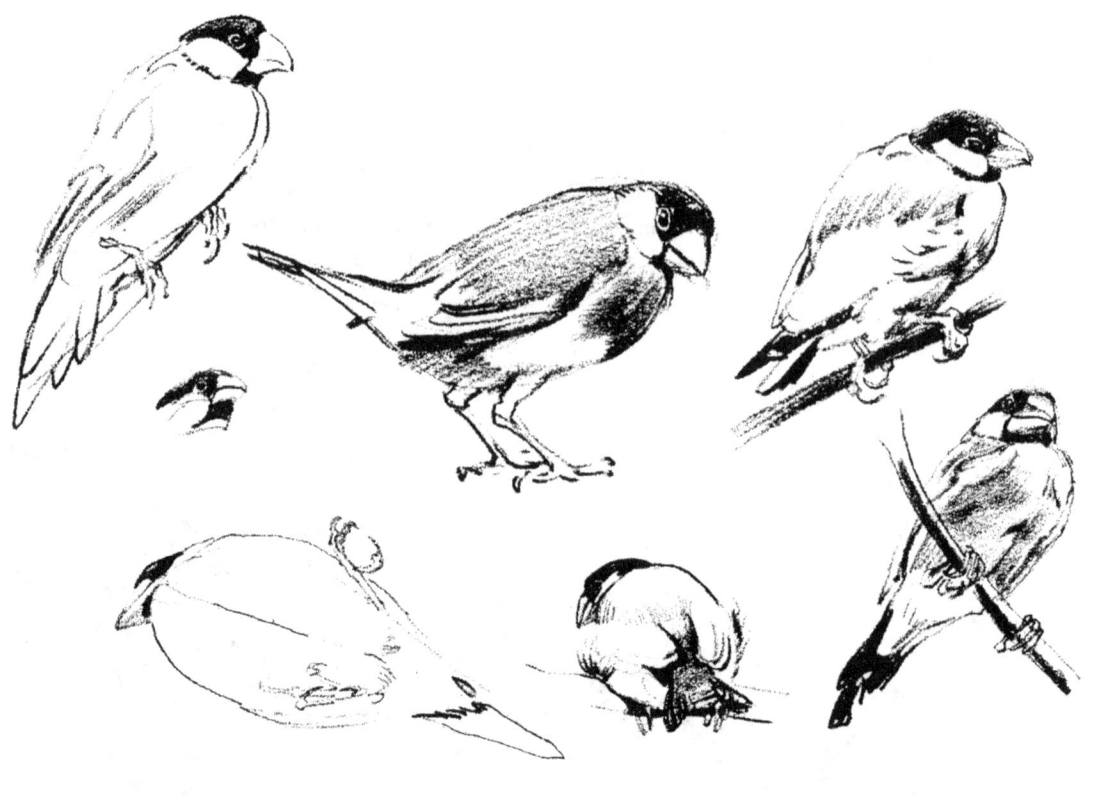

JAVA SPARROWS

I had not drawn this bird before so this page of studies is included to show the importance of drawing birds in many attitudes in order to get to know their shapes properly.

58

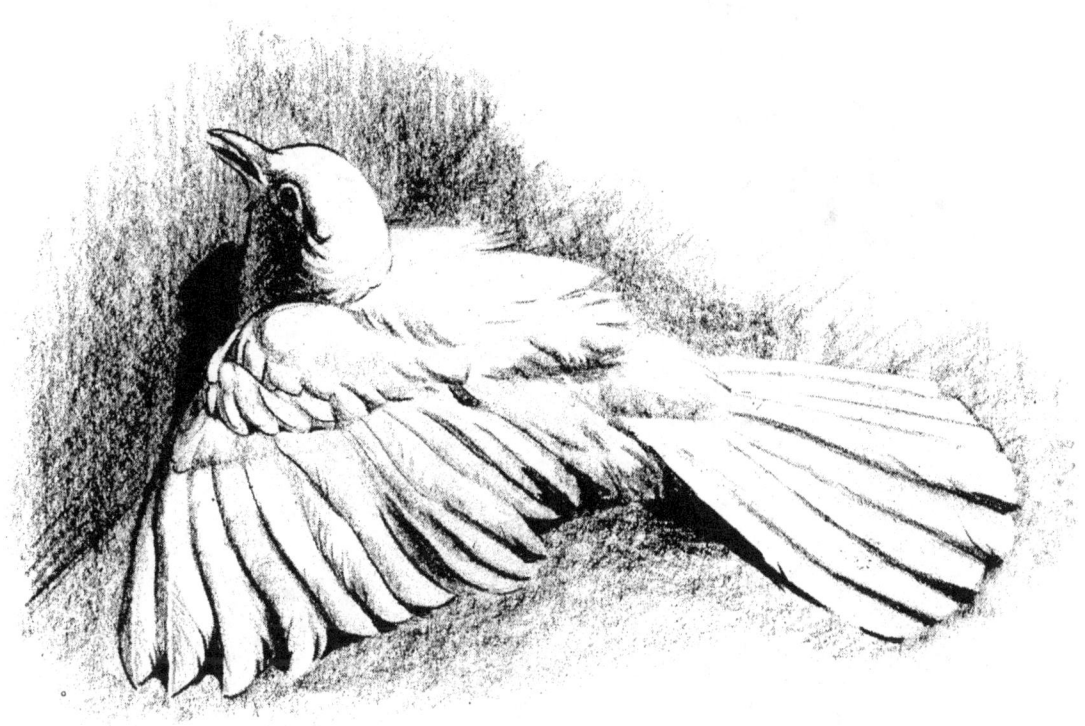

BLACKBIRD

Draw the unexpected offering such as this blackbird basking in the sun. Its outstretched wings gave a unique opportunity for study. Ignore local colour if the structure is what interests you.

Here again, a blackbird stayed in another position just long enough for me to draw the interesting details of wings and tail in this particular attitude.

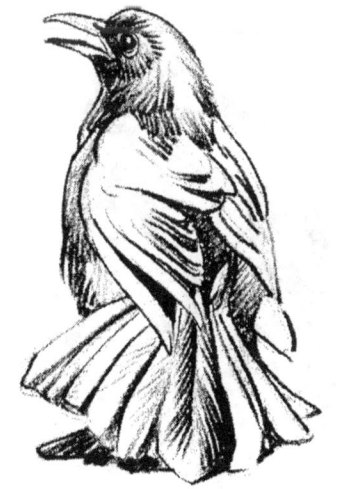

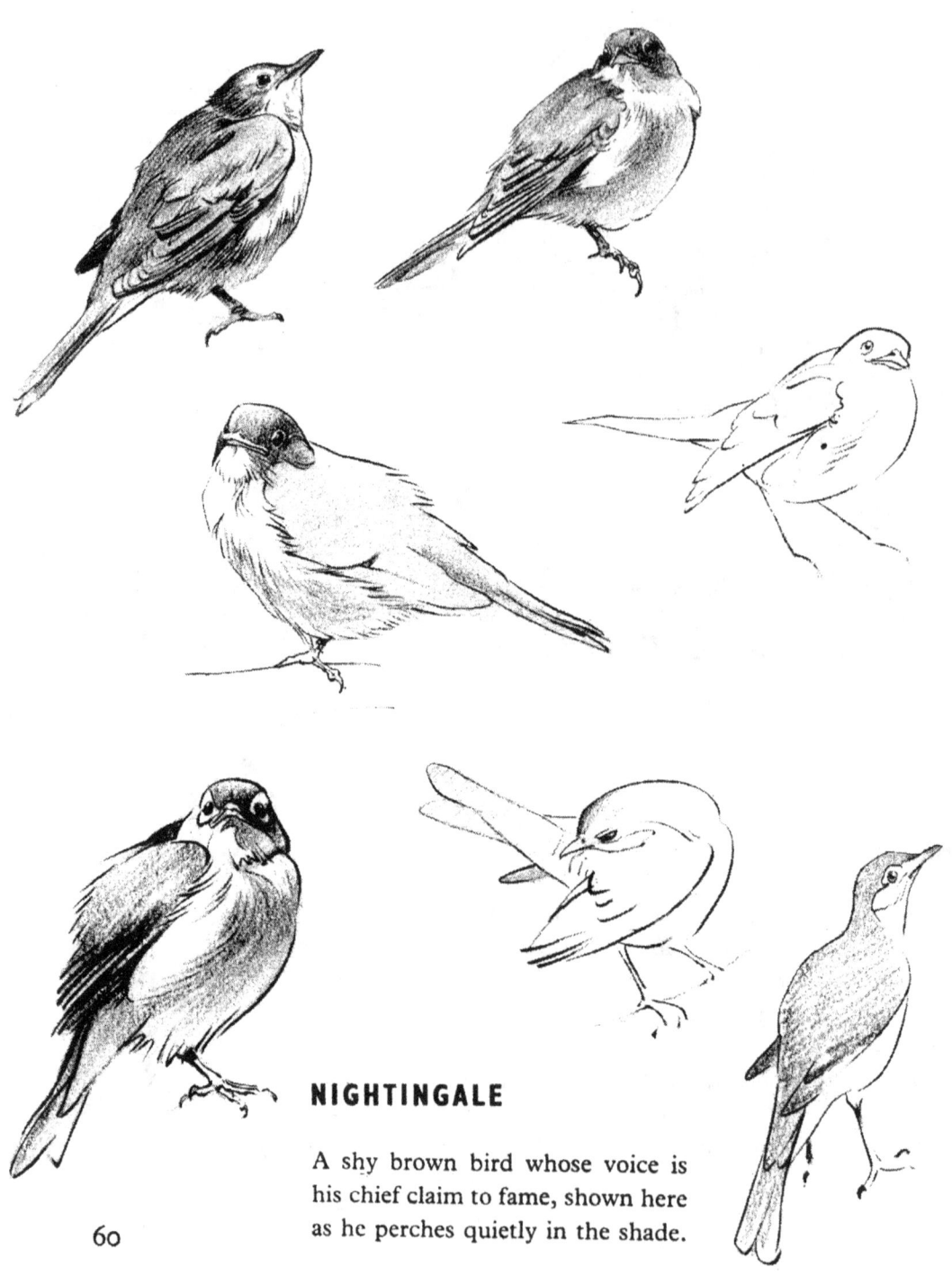

NIGHTINGALE

A shy brown bird whose voice is
his chief claim to fame, shown here
as he perches quietly in the shade.

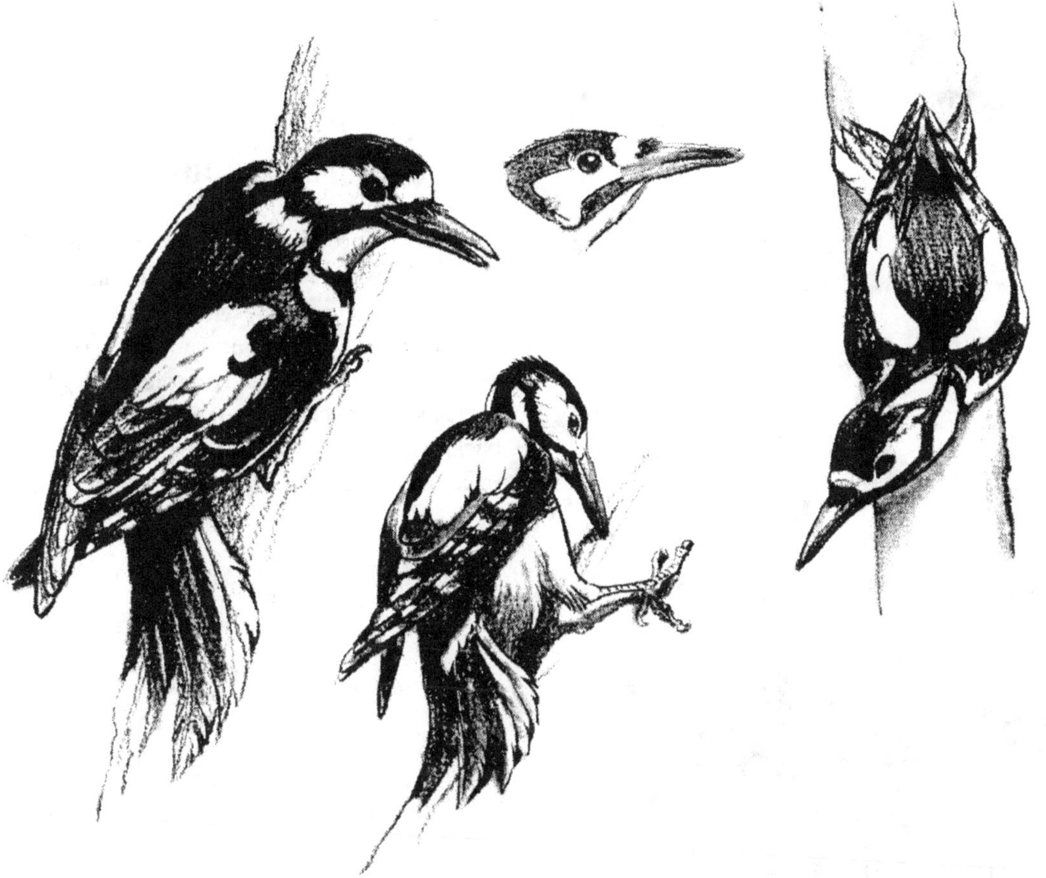

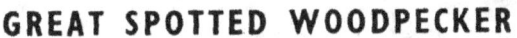

GREAT SPOTTED WOODPECKER

Notice how this bird braces itself against the trunk with its short stiff tail, whilst its zygodactyle or 'yoked' feet (two toes pointing forward, two toes pointing backwards) fairly grips the bark. The lower left study was made from a caged specimen as it clung to the wire. The strong pied pattern is most distinctive and immediately identifies the bird.

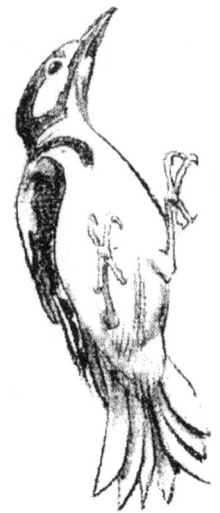

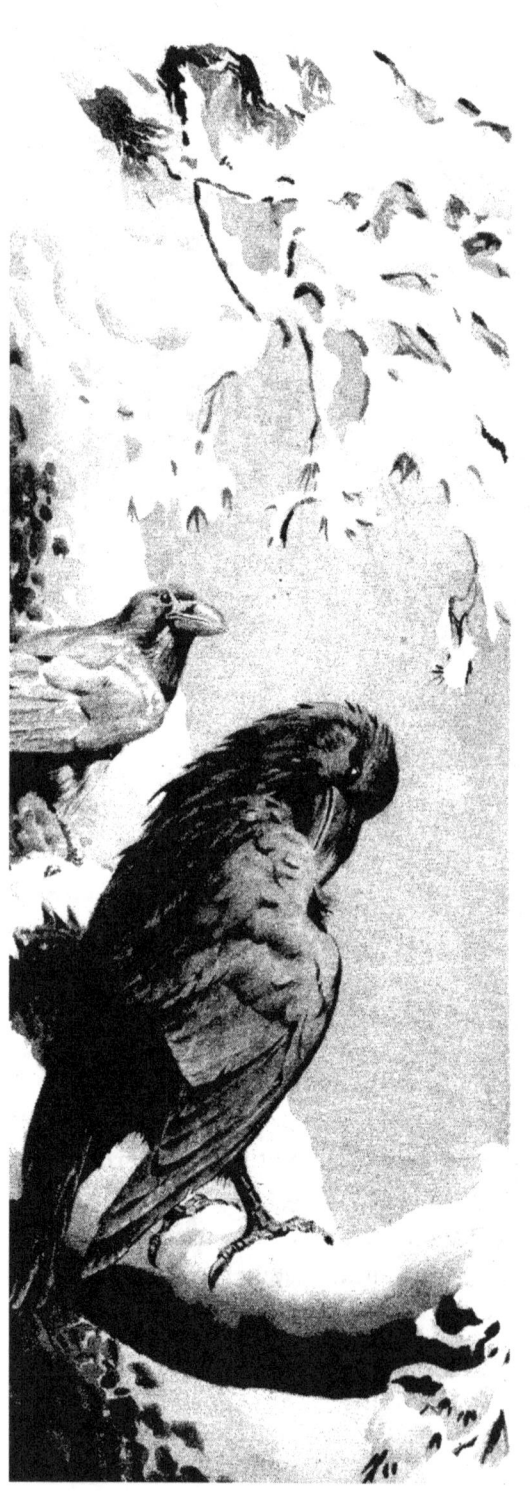

PICTURES FROM YOUR STUDIES

Here is a reproduction of a water colour I made of ravens in the snow. The idea for this picture came to me whilst I was making a study of a raven preening its plumage and reproduced below. I had another study for the second raven. In this case I kept the background tone as quiet as possible so as to centralise the interest on the bird.

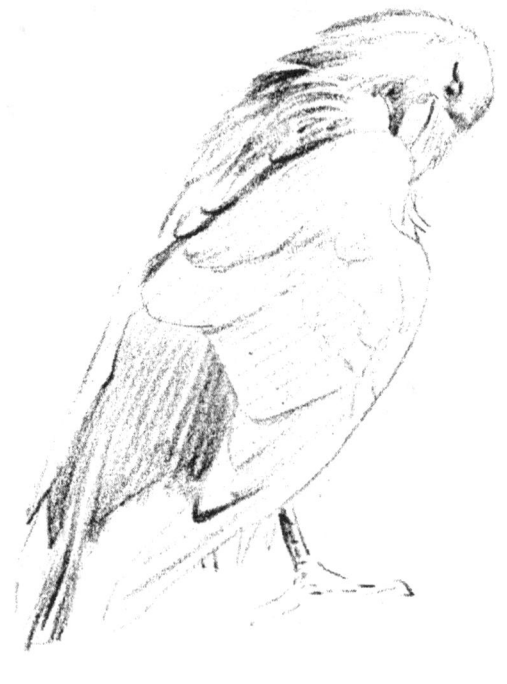

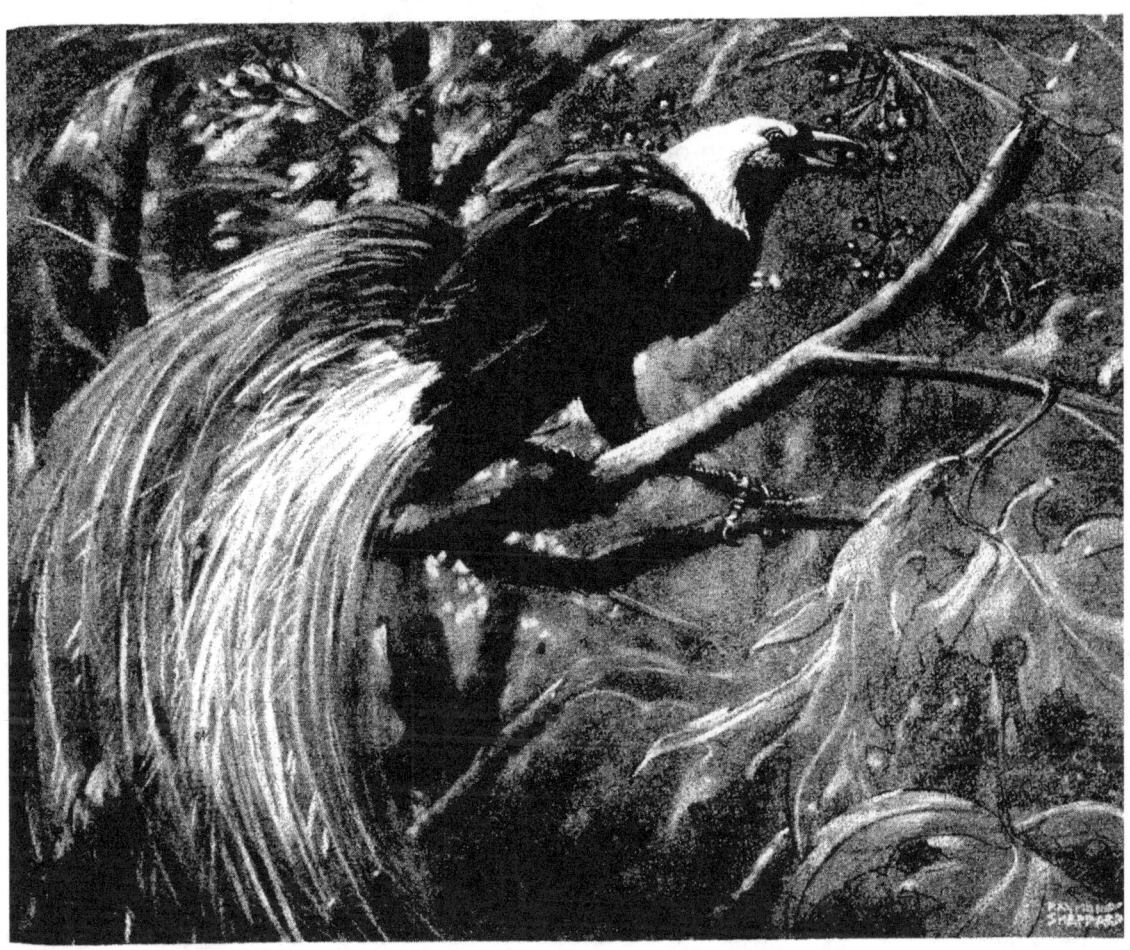

Sometimes one gets the idea for a picture a long time after the study has been made. I keep my studies in easily identified folders so that if the need arises I can look through all the studies, made over a period of time, of one particular species and sort out those necessary to help in composing a picture. This picture of a bird of paradise was done in pastel from the study on page 38. The background was suggested by the tree I drew at Kew Gardens reproduced on page 56.

The background should always be drawn in scale with the bird. A small bird like a wren can be shown amidst a spray of leaves, while an eagle can sit on a great fang of granite with a mountain landscape behind.

As I said at the beginning of this book, there are thousands of birds in the world all infinitely varied and lovely and I hope that after looking through this book you will feel stimulated to go out yourself and find still more birds to draw.

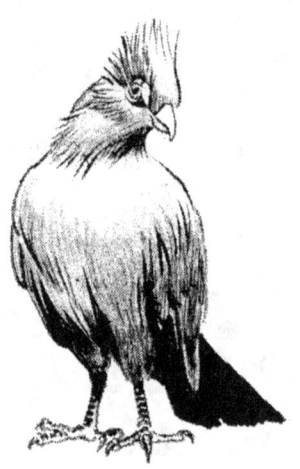

COACHWHIP PUBLICATIONS
CoachwhipBooks.com

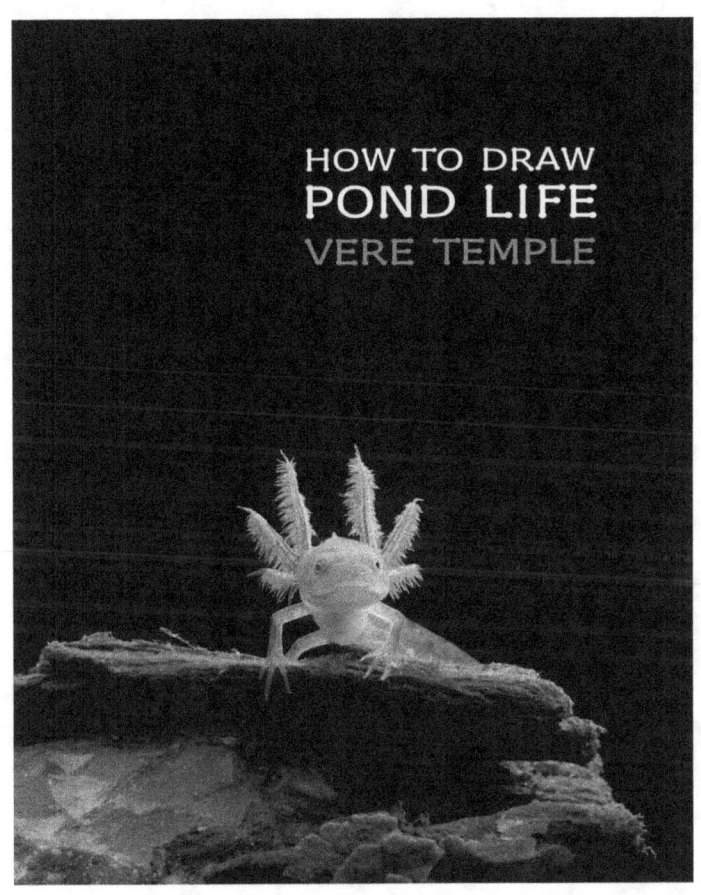

COACHWHIP PUBLICATIONS
CoachwhipBooks.com

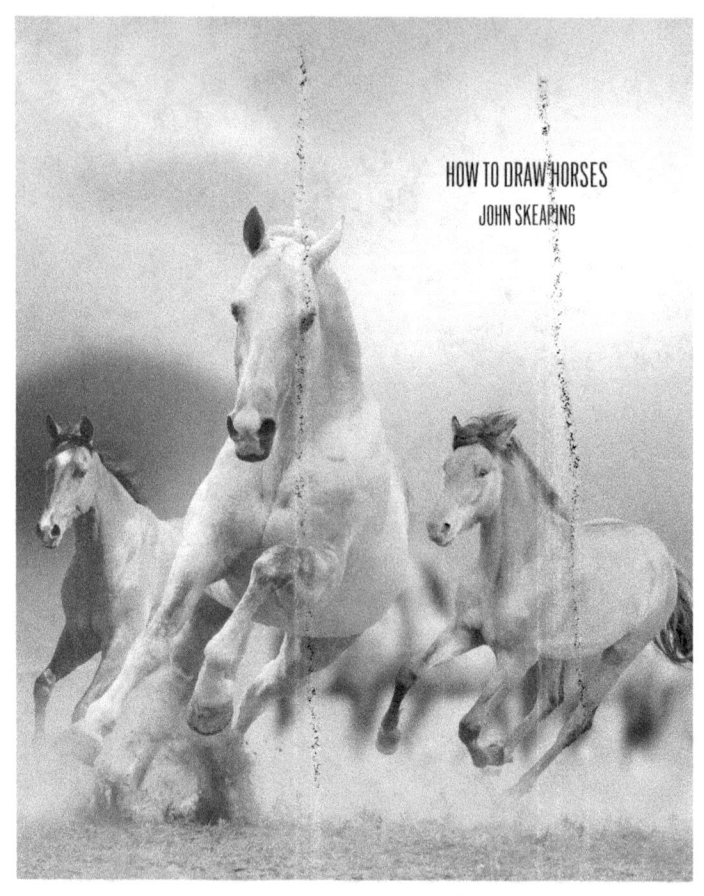

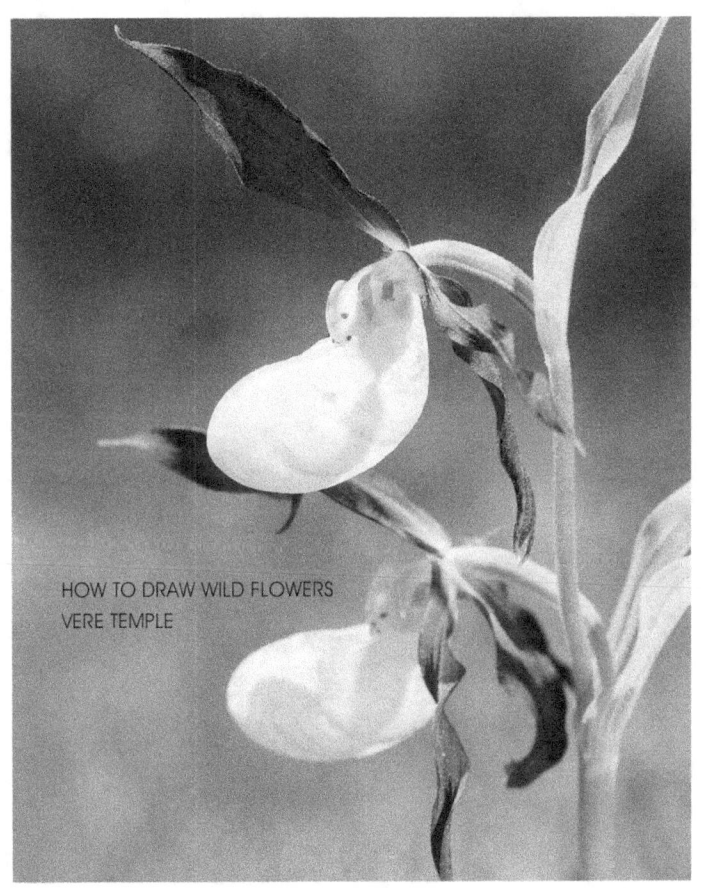

HOW TO DRAW WILD FLOWERS
VERE TEMPLE

COACHWHIP PUBLICATIONS
CoachwhipBooks.com

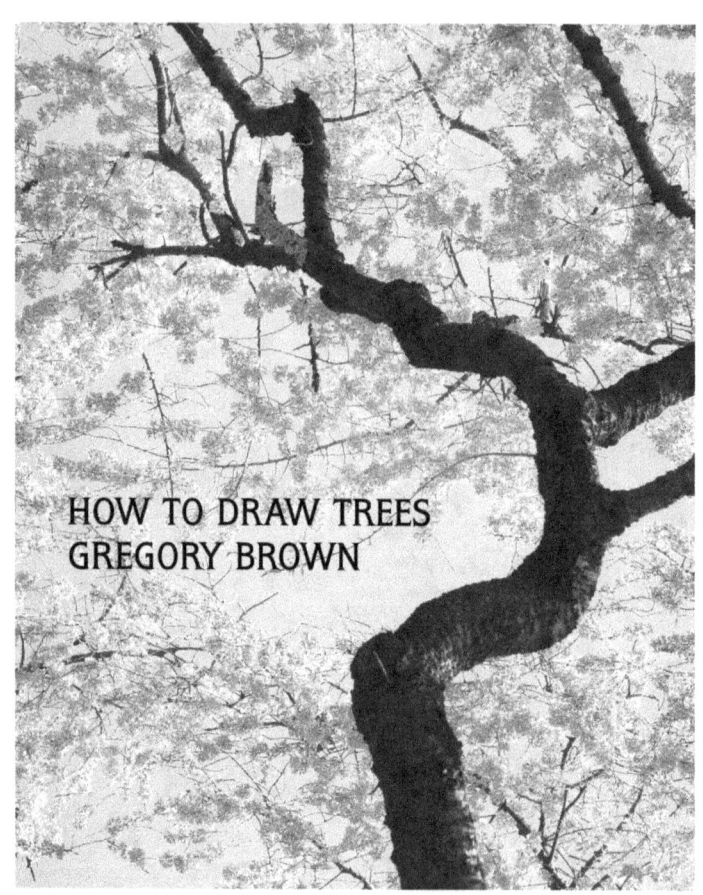

HOW TO DRAW TREES
GREGORY BROWN

COACHWHIP PUBLICATIONS
CoachwhipBooks.com

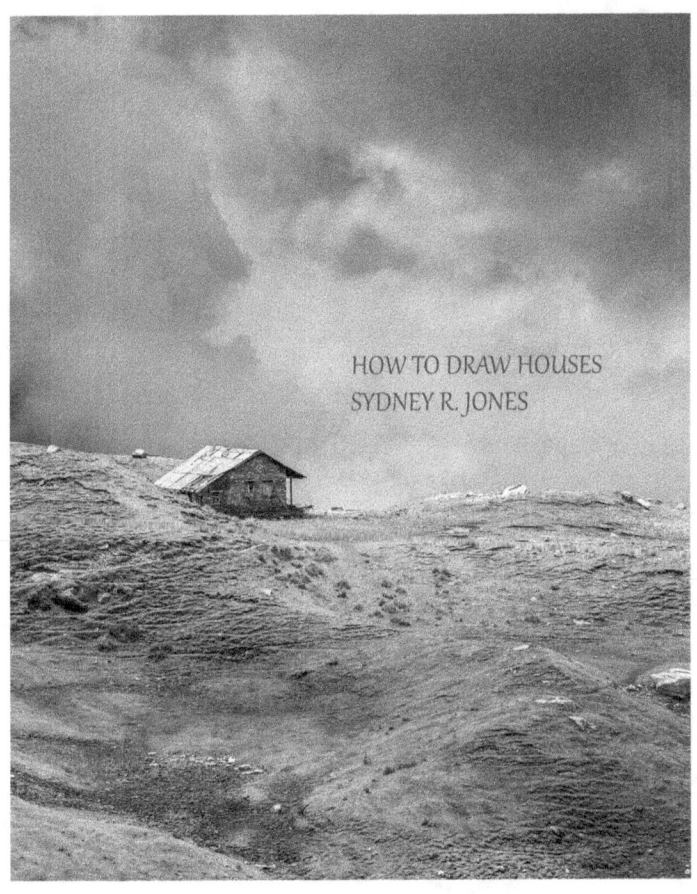

HOW TO DRAW HOUSES
SYDNEY R. JONES

COACHWHIP PUBLICATIONS
CoachwhipBooks.com

TANKS

AND HOW TO DRAW THEM

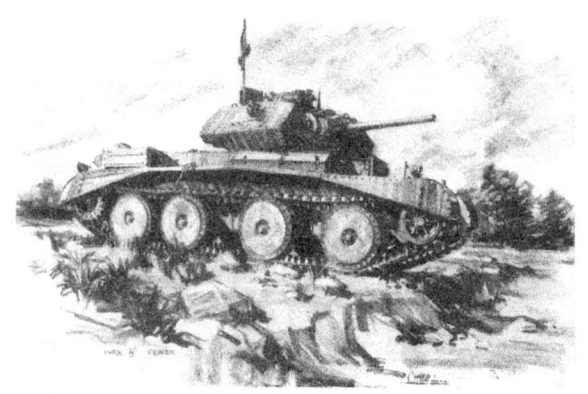

TERENCE T. CUNEO

COACHWHIP PUBLICATIONS
CoachwhipBooks.com

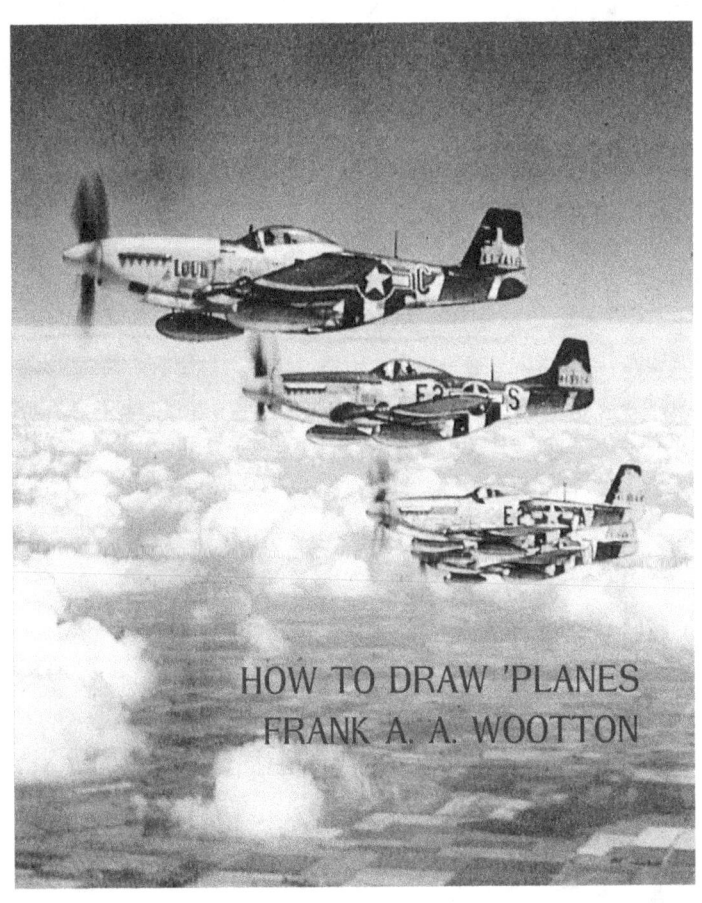

HOW TO DRAW 'PLANES
FRANK A. A. WOOTTON

www.ingramcontent.com/pod-product-compliance
Lightning Source LLC
Chambersburg PA
CBHW081300170526
45165CB00011B/3359